Rescue Your Dog from Fear

Rescue Your Dog from Fear

Tried-and-True Techniques to
Help Your Dog Feel Secure

PEGGY O. SWAGER

Guilford, Connecticut

An imprint of Rowman & Littlefield

Distributed by NATIONAL BOOK NETWORK

British Library Cataloguing-in-Publication information available

Library of Congress Cataloging-in-Publication data available

ISBN 978-1-4930-0477-5 (paperback)
ISBN 978-1-4930-1634-1 (e-book)

♾ ™ The paper used in this publication meets the minimum requirements of American National Standard for Information Sciences—Permanence of Paper for Printed Library Materials, ANSI/NISO Z39.48–1992.

This book is dedicated to my mother
who put up with me
working with so many pets when I was young.
To my husband
who has helped me work with so many dogs,
even though he sometimes got bit,
and to my daughter and son,
Tia Reinschmidt and Scott Olson.
They both are good dog trainers in their own right
and have helped me reform
some of my problematic dogs.

CONTENTS

INTRODUCTION

"He's here in my lap as we speak, and I think he knows you've called," Jina told me when I rang her to get an update on Albert. The long-haired Chihuahua now owns Jina. I knew he'd be the one to own her and not the other way around. They'd hit it off when she came to meet my foster dog, as if they were destined to be together. Jina then told me about teatime, where Albert's tail spins like a helicopter as she takes down his cup and places a bone in it. He'd then politely follow her to the table and join her and her son for the tea ceremony. No wonder they gave him the nickname "Sir Albert."

For many people, this kind of cute behavior in a dog is coveted. Seeing Albert now, it may be hard to envision his life before. Two years earlier, Albert was a highly fearful dog living in a mill dog rescue. After spending a year at the facility, even though the dog was on anxiety medication, the rescue worried he would be unadoptable. When I first took on Albert as a foster dog, he was so fearful that he'd curl up into a ball and go into a catatonic state when people tried to interact with him. When he came out of that highly fearful state, sometimes he'd bite.

With the right techniques, Albert was able to transform from a mill dog to a regular dog.

Otis was another dog at the mill dog rescue I fostered because he wasn't able to transition from the mill dog environment to a regular home without help. He is now a confident dog. I remember when I took him to a friend's house whose father was in a wheelchair. Otis went up to the guy with his tail wagging as if he was a therapy dog.

I've had the privilege of helping out a lot of fearful and highly fearful dogs. Some were mill dog rescues, some came from regular rescues, and others were pets owned by people for years. Nothing is more rewarding than to see these dogs go from timid to enjoying their lives like any other dog.

Albert is a dog who illustrates that you can rescue your dog from fear, even if he was raised breaking all the rules for developing security in a dog. Up until four years of age, Albert lived in constant fear, especially when it came to interacting with people. Yet he recovered from his fear issues. This book works to give all dog owners the tools they need to help their dog feel safe and secure. Issues from house-training regression to submissive peeing are covered extensively. Dog owners who have pets with fear issues will learn about mistakes they may be making that can contribute to their dog's lack of security. Becoming your dog's fear advocate can help your dog learn to trust you and keep the dog out of harmful situations.

Fearful dogs need confidence to become less fearful. Ways to do that include establishing a foundation of security in your dog, finding out how to be a dependable leader to your dog, and learning the best possible techniques for desensitizing the dog. The firsthand stories of successes with reforming fearful dogs will not only present solutions for people with similar issues, but can also give hope to all dog owners.

CHAPTER 1

Where Do Fearful Dogs Come From?

Although, in essence, fear is a healthy reaction to the threat of danger, some people are having issues because the dog is reacting to a nonthreatening situation or the dog is overreacting. If your dog is too often or too intensely afraid of too many things, you have a problem that needs to be fixed. Overly fearful dogs may be afraid of most people, other dogs, things, noises, or places. These dogs can be skittish on walks and may react to noises other dogs ignore. Dogs with fear issues may hide from people coming over to your house. The same dog may panic if you leave its side, making the dog more prone to separation anxiety. Excessive fearfulness in dogs can result in behavior issues from house-training problems to aggression. Without the right kind of intervention, a dog's fearfulness and insecurity can grow. A good place to begin to help a dog with fear issues is to learn where fear in dogs comes from.

FEARFULNESS IN DOGS

There are a multitude of reasons why you see fearfulness in dogs. Certain base personalities in dogs can pose more of a challenge to a dog's sense of security, including shyness, a reserved nature, and a highly sensitive nature. Under-socializing a dog can generate a fearful animal. Dogs with more challenging personalities or behavior problems due to fear are at a greater risk of being surrendered as a rescue. Unfortunately, most dogs find a rescue environment stressful, creating fear in dogs who didn't

1

previously have issues and compounding fear in those who did. Some fearful dogs are created when we misunderstand or miscommunicate with them when asking for compliance, especially if harsh training techniques are used.

Talking Terms

Often, we interchange the words *shyness* and *fearfulness*. We often describe fearful dogs as acting shy. Below are some working definitions of those terms.

- Fear: the emotion experienced in the presence or threat of danger. Fear is a vital response to physical and emotional danger.

- Fearfulness: feeling or inclined to feel anxiety or apprehension; timid; nervous.

- Shyness: fearful shyness typically begins when the animal is young. Shyness involves being frightened in social situations or being frightened when with others. The feeling of apprehension can range from mild to extreme.

WHERE FEARFUL OR SHY DOGS COME FROM

Dogs who are shy by nature, or have a reserved nature, are prone to becoming fearful and will require specialized training and handling to counter that issue. Another trait that can cause or add to fear issues is a highly sensitive nature. A highly sensitive dog may become uncertain about various stimuli such as loud noises or even people sneezing. These dogs can remain fearful if they are not helped to understand their environment. A soft dog is a dog who seems to take sensitivity to an extreme. These dogs become very uncomfortable with direct eye contact and often find verbal reprimands too harsh.

If your dog is either shy or reserved, you need to identify that trait. If the dog is highly sensitive or soft, recognizing that attribute can help you take actions to create a more secure dog. But keep in mind that dogs who are shy or reserved can also be highly sensitive or soft, making them more of a challenge.

Under-socializing a dog can create shyness in a dog. Dogs need to be socialized, or introduced to things in our world in the right way, so they understand this is not something to react fearfully about. Dogs who do not have adequate socialization can react fearfully when there is no real threat to them.

THE NATURE OF SHY DOGS

Shy dogs are not naturally comfortable in the world. These dogs display fear of things they are not familiar with, including people they have not met. They can quickly become insecure in an unfamiliar place. These dogs prefer to retreat rather than take time to size up the situation to determine if they are safe. For that reason, they prefer a very limited world rather than an expanded one.

For example, although a shy dog may love to go for walks, if a stranger is encountered (some dogs are shy around humans while others are shy around dogs, and some are shy around both), the dog will want to flee or escape. This issue is even more pronounced if the dog is already uncertain when walking with you. Some dogs may be uncertain when escorting you on a walk because they don't see you as a strong leader. We all feel more secure and safe with a strong leader.

Shy dogs can vary in their degree of shyness. Some are a little timid, while others are extreme. The relationship with the dog owner can either diminish the dog's shyness or increase it. Owners who show good leadership reassure their fearful dogs by their mere presence. Owners who coddle their fearful dogs can actually perpetuate their fears. Even if the owner has the best intentions for the dog, if the owner doesn't take the correct actions, the dog will become more insecure.

Shyness Triggers

Although the primary information in this book is geared towards dogs who are shy around other people, dogs can also be shy or uncertain about other dogs or other animals they have not previously encountered. Many of the techniques used for dogs who are shy around people can be adapted for dogs who are insecure about other dogs.

Organically Shy Dogs

Just as some people are more timid or shy by nature, so are some dogs. This kind of shyness has genetic roots. The degree to which the dog is shy can also vary. Some dogs are a little timid and can more readily be socialized into pets who are not timid. Other dogs are severely shy and although they can learn to survive in our world, at times they will need our help. Even with the right kind of work, shy dogs typically keep a part of that shyer nature, and that nature can resurface at times when they feel less comfortable. Those times include going to an unfamiliar place or the dog's being asked to interact with too many unfamiliar people.

Dogs with genetic roots for shyness can be a result of a faulty breeding program. Most breed standards in purebreds discourage the breeding of shyer animals and fault this trait in purebred dogs. Unfortunately, some dogs may be bred in spite of their shyness issues. For example, herding dogs are bred to strategically chase after an animal and to work with a dog handler. Sometimes, a more timid nature towards people seems to get attached to the desired traits in the working dog. You now have a dog breeder who has the choice of culling a great herding champion because the dog is timid around strangers, or breeding in hopes the unwanted shyness won't be passed along. Often, that shyness is retained along with the desired traits.

Ribbons or working abilities are not the only reasons a shyer dog may be bred. One breeder of miniature Australian shepherds had repeat customers. The pups were shyer, although not extreme. Some of her clients liked the idea because the dogs were more clingy to their owners. The owners mistook that overly dependent nature in the dog for love. The truth of the matter is that dogs will love you to their fullest extent if they are given a chance. And, overdependence is not real love. The other problem is that although some people like this trait, too many of the dogs with this issue end up in animal shelters because this problem can keep a pet from being enjoyable unless the dog is kept isolated inside the house. Dogs who are overly dependent are also more prone to separation anxiety.

Nutritional deficiencies in very young dogs can create organic shyness. In the book *The Dog's Mind*, authors Bruce Fogle and Anne B. Wilson talk about how nutritional deficiencies in very young puppies resulted in extreme shyness in the adult dogs. Several rescues who had come from an Indian reservation were notably shy, and at the heart of their problem was poor nutrition. When these dogs were very young, there was no adequate nutrition available for the underweight mother, resulting in severe nutritional deficiencies in the puppies. These puppies grew into shy adults, even though the dogs were worked for socialization in a rescue.

I had firsthand experience with organic shyness in some Jack Russell terriers, also known as Parson Russell terriers. Two dogs my daughter and I owned, Alexis and Cookie, came from a litter where the mother dog quit producing milk when the puppies were two days old. The first day or so of trying to bottle-feed the litter didn't go well. Even though things did improve by the end of the week, these two puppies were the thinnest ones in the litter, with Alexis being worse. All the puppies were shyer, and the degree of shyness correlated to how thin the puppies were that first week of life.

WHAT IS A RESERVED DOG?

Shy dogs and reserved dogs are different in nature. A shy dog seems born with a tendency to find the world fearful. Without work, the dog will remain very afraid of most things and may take a long time to leave the fear state once he becomes fearful. A reserved dog seems born with a sense of caution. That cautious nature means the dog will want to evaluate a person or situation before feeling safe. Since this kind of dog needs more time than other dogs to evaluate things before proceeding, the more socialization you do with a reserved dog, the more readily the dog can decide a certain situation or certain people are not a threat. Once the dog decides someone isn't a threat, he will warm up to that person much like a normal dog. However, if you don't allow the dog to feel comfortable, he can begin to react fearfully.

Reserved Dog Rules

Reserved dogs have a set of rules for engagement. A lot of these rules also work for organically shy dogs. When you first approach a reserved dog, you need to stop at a proper social distance. This distance is typically a few feet away and is noted by the dog becoming uncertain when you cross that invisible threshold. Uncertain dogs may become still, tense, or even take a step backwards. They may even turn their head sideways. If you don't take the dog's hint, the reserved dog will take evasive actions, resembling a shyer dog.

With reserved dogs, if you stay at their socially comfortable distance and give them time to decide if you pose a threat or not, they will often relax about your presence. Once the dog relaxes, many times the dog will approach you. If not, you can try lowering to the dog's level to ask the dog for a greeting.

To greet a reserved dog, keep in mind some of them don't like a hand coming over the top of their head. However, most will welcome a rub on their chest. Typically, if you approach a reserved dog correctly, the dog will welcome attention.

Consequences of Approaching a Reserved Dog the Wrong Way

My daughter's dog, Arwin, is a reserved dog. When I took Arwin to the vet for her rabies shot, my regular vet was not available, so I agreed to see the "newer" veterinarian at the office. To the vet's credit, he attempted to put my dog at ease by getting down on the floor to greet her. But then, he made the mistake of trying to pet her on the head. For her, that was a deal breaker for trusting him. That kind of action is the wrong protocol for a reserved dog who just met someone new. In addition, Arwin was already ill at ease because she was at the vet's.

There were two ways things could have played out from that point. Many reserved dogs, when at a veterinary office, become so stressed that they bite or snap at the vet, especially during the exam. Already stressed, dogs may react poorly when a vet gets personal by looking into ears and pulling back gums, not to mention taking the dog's temperature. Since the vet had already put Arwin off by trying to pet her on the head before she felt comfortable with him, things could have gone poorly during the visit, especially when he stuck her with a needle. However, I took actions to get Arwin to relax before that shot.

The first thing I did was get the vet to quickly abandon the head pet and rub Arwin's chest instead. I also used the word "easy." Arwin has learned to relax when I say that word. I talk in chapter eight about teaching a dog to relax with this word. Arwin also trusted me as well as saw me as a leader. And lastly, since I acted calm about this situation, Arwin drew on that calm and her trust in me, allowing her to get through the appointment without incident.

Herding Breeds

The majority of the reserved dogs I have encountered come from herding breeds. Border collies can be reserved or shy, and I've met a lot of reserved shelties (Shetland sheepdogs). The shelties were very social and friendly if you gave them a chance, but they needed to take that first step towards you. I also noted that the shelties tended to remember me and not be as reserved the next time. Arwin is an English shepherd, a less-known herding breed.

A CONTRACT WITH YOUR SHY OR RESERVED DOG

Though you can socialize many shy and most reserved dogs to the point they feel comfortable in most places and situations, you never change a dog's base nature. Therefore, you need to become the dog's advocate when needed. In a way, you enter into a contract with the dog that allows the dog to feel comfortable in situations where he, by nature, may become fearful.

The first part of that contract has already been mentioned. You need to prove your trustworthiness through good leadership. Reserved and shy dogs, by nature, will have doubts and concerns about some people, and they will need to take your word on what is okay and what is not. Your leadership is earned through training and the correct interactions with the dog, which is discussed in more detail in chapter nine.

The second part of the contract is that you will intervene on your dog's behalf. If someone is walking directly towards your dog, already reaching out with that hand to land atop the dog's head, you need to step in between your dog and that person. Although some reserved and shy dogs are fine with being patted on top of their heads, that kind of contact will only be allowed once the dog has had ample time to decide a person in this situation is okay to interact with. So when people approach your dog, look for those subtle signs of discomfort in your dog that tell you that you need to step in.

Some of the early signs include the dog tensing, turning his head, or moving away from the approaching person, and the dog leaning backwards when the person gets closer. Sometimes the dog will stare at the person as if trying to size the person up. Other times the dog may glance towards you for guidance. If the dog is looking for guidance, help him to feel more secure by either intervention or verbal reassurance.

Once a hesitant dog has had a chance to relax, most prefer being petted on the chest or under the chin as the first place of contact. If your dog is that way, you need to guide people in that direction.

Be aware that shy or reserved dogs may begin to feel insecure in unfamiliar places. Learn to pick up on when your dog is feeling insecure. Sometimes when a dog goes somewhere he isn't familiar with, the dog begins to show hesitation when walking, may have his tail down, and may spend a lot of time looking around nervously. If your dog is already uncertain, be cautious about asking him to be social in this kind of situation.

Some dogs seem to have a short social saturation point. If your dog no longer shows interest in being touched by people, intervene on your dog's behalf.

If the dog becomes overwhelmed in a situation for any reason, remove the dog to a quiet and secure place and allow him to regain his composure. However, if at all possible, don't leave the facility while the dog is in an insecure state. That can confirm to the dog that this situation is one that he needs to flee, thus reinforcing the dog's insecurity. Once the dog regains his composure and you have the opportunity to leave, do so. If it is not possible to leave, work to keep the dog from again feeling overwhelmed. Dogs who feel secure in a crate can be crated in a quiet corner. Do not expect the dog to want to meet anyone.

A critical part of the contract is that you will adequately and correctly socialize the dog. For the most part, you can use the same process to socialize your reserved dog as you do any dog. However, you need to keep a couple things in mind. First, you need to take things at the dog's pace, even though that pace may not be the same as for other dogs. And second, even a well-socialized reserved dog may regress if the dog encounters something that causes uncertainty in him. Don't worry if you can't figure out why the dog is acting uncertain. The goal is to learn to respect your dog's limits. Dogs can have a bad day. Don't push your dog past his limits.

THE SENSITIVE DOG

I've mentioned that a dog who is sensitive can be more challenging. The two major sensitivities that cause issues in dogs are overreaction to stimuli such as noises and oversensitivity to human emotions. Soft dogs are dogs who overreact to pressure from people. These dogs are an extreme form of sensitive dog. When a sensitive dog overreacts, the dog often becomes fearful.

Noise-Sensitive Dogs

One of the most common kinds of stimuli that can create issues in more sensitive dogs is noise. Some dogs are very sensitive to loud or strange noises. The noises make them startle, and the dog often feels insecure or fearful afterwards. Noises that are coupled with other frightening stimuli can have an additive effect, creating a greater fear response. This is talked about more in chapter ten. Dogs who are more sensitive to noises may make an association with other things they are uncertain about, creating a separate fear from the noise. One of the problems with noise-sensitive dogs is that the dog reacts poorly to a noise stimulus, and if the dog owner doesn't work with the dog to get over the noise sensitivity, the dog's apprehension can grow, resulting in more insecurity and fearfulness in the dog.

Sensitive to Reprimands

Some dog are more sensitive to verbal reprimands. One of the reasons the dog may be sensitive to a reprimand is that the dog is adversely reacting to a negative human emotion such as anger, which often accompanies our disapproval. Tone of voice can often trigger a fearful reaction, including too energetic of a tone when the dog is already insecure.

What may surprise some people is what a dog considers a harsh reprimand. For some dogs, a stern "no" is too much for them. What also may shock people is that sometimes a more defiant and strong-willed dog may be sensitive to verbal reprimands. Although the dog may not do anything you ask, if you use too harsh of a tone of voice, the dog will act as if your discipline was too harsh. Even though you may not see your stern "no" as harsh at all, you need to identify if your dog responds as if the tone is too harsh. Dogs reacting poorly to reprimands are more prone to become insecure or fearful, especially since this can deteriorate the human-leadership bond.

Some of the subtle signs that a dog is responding poorly to your reprimands include offering overly submissive behaviors such as rolling onto his back at your approach. The dog may also offer appeasing behaviors such as crawling towards you or away from you as the dog tries to calm down your emotional state. Some dogs will act as if you have harmed them somehow by giving you a pained look. Watch out for head lowering, or ears going back, or the tail dropping. All three may be present. Some dogs may even cringe as if you were trying to hit them. It doesn't matter that you never hit the dog or threaten him, if the dog is sensitive to reprimands, he is going to react.

Another problem with dogs who are sensitive to reprimands is that they have a hard time associating the reprimand with the unwanted behavior. The dog too often gets so caught up with his reaction that your point is lost. Typically dogs that do this are having a hard time dealing with your emotional response. Since dogs who are overly sensitive to reprimands often are focused on you and your disapproval rather than changing the unwanted behavior, you need to avoid or soften your disapproval. A good approach to the problem is for you to learn to teach the dog the behavior you do want, rather than work to discipline the behavior you don't want.

A Defiant but Sensitive Dog

Lestat, a terrier, was quite strong-willed. He preferred to do things his way as well as seemed to enjoy blowing off commands. He was trained to do agility, and at first he did a stellar job. But then, he must have found this task boring (not unusual in this breed) because if you gave him a command a second late, he'd go off and make up his own course.

I worked with this dog to try to help turn around his attitude, but I confess, I made a mistake at first. As willful as this dog was, I didn't expect him to be sensitive to reprimands at all. However, when I was practicing him on weaving through poles, he missed one of the weaves. I told him "no," and although I didn't say it sternly, he must have felt I'd used too much force. Soon, Lestat began to quit in the middle of competitions and run off the course. Fortunately, one day another trainer watching me work the dog noted that when I corrected Lestat using the word "no," his ears lowered and his tail dropped. To get this dog back on track, I learned to ask him in a motivational tone to repeat an obstacle or a command, rather than tell him he did something wrong.

Pushy Dogs Can Also Be Sensitive

A pushy dog is like a pushy salesman. They know they are over-stepping their boundaries and breaking rules, but they have an agenda, and it is in their nature to put that agenda first. The sensitive yet pushy dog lives in a paradox. The dog is very insensitive to you and your wishes, yet if you reprimand him, the dog can be hypersensitive to that reprimand. This confounds a lot of dog owners in that they can't understand how a dog who is clearly acting "dominant" and "alpha" has this kind of problem. A lot of the owners' confusion is generated by the tendency to label about any kind of dog behavior problem as the dog being either dominant or alpha, or both. These traits seldom drive a dog's misbehaviors. In fact, the terms have become so misused that they no longer accurately describe behavior issues.

The other problem with dogs sensitive to human reprimands, as mentioned earlier, is that they don't make the connection between physical and harsh punishment and the reason you are punishing them. Instead, the dog takes your reprimand about as well as you would take your best friend hauling off and slapping you over a simple misunderstanding. Some dogs depend heavily on the dog-human relationship for compliance, and if you come across as too harsh to such sensitive dogs, you injure that very important relationship.

Not all pushy dogs are highly sensitive to human emotions, such as our anger. I've seen many Rottweilers, pit bulls, and Jack Russell terriers be both pushy and highly sensitive. However, I worked with a very pushy Chesapeake Bay retriever mix who was not sensitive to reprimands. That didn't give me much of an advantage. Reprimands still didn't change her unwanted jumping up. Fortunately, the correct training did solve her misbehaviors. In general, training a dog to do an action you want rather than reprimanding for behaviors you don't want provides a better solution to behavior problems.

Sensitivity to More Than Reprimands

Anger and disapproval are not the only emotions I've seen highly sensitive dogs react to. I've also known dogs who can't tolerate people who are nervous. I knew of a dog who'd passed all her disposition tests at the shelter with flying colors. When I encountered the dog a year later, she was fearful and aggressive. What I discovered was that the dog owner was always stressed out and this dog was unable to tolerate the constant nervousness in the owner. The net result was a very fearful dog who turned aggressive.

For some dogs, our sadness might be disturbing. I've also observed a dog respond aggressively towards a child who was hyperactive. The dog was not aggressive by nature, but didn't understand the erratic actions of this child. Ironically, that same pushy Chesapeake Bay retriever mix I mentioned earlier was later adopted by this family. The pushy retriever had no problems with the hyperactivity in the child. But then, the dog was a bit hyperactive herself.

If you find your dog is beginning to act reserved, fearful, or stressed in a situation, check to see how you are feeling emotionally. If the dog is acting uncertain about a particular person, determine if the person is displaying emotions the dog is not comfortable with.

SOFT DOGS

Soft dogs take sensitivity to reprimands to an extreme. These dogs are very reactive to pressure, and that reactivity can result in a perpetual state of fear in them. Pressure to these dogs may include people approaching too directly, as well as any kind of physical interaction by people they are not totally comfortable about, such as touch. These dogs often have very little tolerance for direct eye contact. A soft dog is so sensitive to people, he often wants to withdraw from the world.

I remember one soft dog who withdrew to the back of the crate when I glanced in her direction. Yet this kelpie, owned by a herding dog trainer, when in a herding competition was bold with the livestock as well as interacted very well with her owner. This dog is a good example of how some dogs can do certain tasks with confidence and still be very insecure in other situations. Often those other situations involve dealing with people the dog doesn't know or the dog feeling uncomfortable in a situation she is unfamiliar with. Shy dogs, reserved dogs, sensitive dogs, and especially soft dogs, without proper handling, can become very fearful about most things in the world.

Incorrect handing of a softer dog can bring unwanted reactions that may create fear in a dog. One experienced dog owner had a papillon she'd worked to socialize from the time the dog was a puppy. However, when the experienced owner had the dog in an obedience training class, the instructor believed in using a choke collar to apply leash corrections (a quick, often forceful jerk on a leash) to get a dog to heel correctly. Although this technique is still employed by some, it is out of date and not very effective. When the papillon forged ahead of the owner on the walk, the owner gave the dog a jerk on the leash to correct him. Instead of returning to the owner's side, the dog stopped all together and crouched. The instructor encouraged the owner to lighten up but persist with the leash correction. That didn't stop the dog from forging; however, the dog began to show reluctance about walking on the leash in the class. Fortunately, the owner was wise enough to realize that persisting with this technique could end up creating a dog who was apprehensive and fearful. She successfully switched to luring the dog with a treat to learn the correct heel position, and the dog again became confident in classes.

You need to identify the soft dog trait as early as possible. These dogs will show their reactive side while still in the litter. While other puppies may bound forward, these dogs avoid eye

15

contact and will retreat at your approach. If you are a dog breeder, you can help these puppies by working with them one-on-one. Stroke the pup under the chin to help build confidence. Handle the soft dog every day, working or playing with the dog until he becomes comfortable with you and learns to make eye contact. As the dog grows, work on confidence building. Expose the dog to new things and new places a little at a time. Make sure the dog has time to feel comfortable before you move on to a new place or event. Soft dogs need a lot of confidence building.

SHYNESS FROM UNDER-SOCIALIZATION
Under-socialization can result in a dog becoming fearful or shy. At the heart of this problem is a lack of understanding of what is necessary to adequately socialize a dog. Any dog needs a certain amount of socialization, and some dogs need more, depending on their personality. There is an ideal time to begin the dog's social experience, and the rule of thumb is that the earlier in life you start, the better. In fact, a good breeder makes sure the puppies have contact with a variety of people as soon as the pups' eyes open. Without adequate socialization, shy dogs become progressively fearful. The next chapter tells you more about how to adequately socialize your dog.

FEARFULNESS CREATED IN A RESCUE ENVIRONMENT
Rescues have the best intentions for dogs. Some are no-kill facilities and some are not. All rescues and shelters work to find dogs a forever home. Unfortunately, with the excess of dogs, that isn't always possible. Some dogs who go into shelters will not come out. Among the top reasons are aggression, fearfulness, and health issues. Another problem that lurks inside shelters is that some dogs find being kenneled in a shelter environment so stressful that they become unstable.

Dogs who enter into shelters come from all kinds of backgrounds. Often, the lack of training lands the dog on the unwanted list. As you will discover in the chapter on leadership, training can help build security in a dog. Dogs lacking good training are more prone to insecurity in a shelter. However, even a more secure dog can become unstable in this environment. One humane society noted that even dogs they temperament-tested could have this problem. After three weeks, the dogs became stressed out in the kennel environment and began to show behavior issues such as reactivity to noises and people passing by their pens. Some began to pace or spin. Unfortunately, once these dogs took up those kinds of behaviors, the humane society viewed them as too unlikely for adoption. As well, they had other dogs coming in who needed a chance at a home.

Many rescues depend heavily upon foster care to home dogs waiting for adoption. Foster care is often a better situation for a dog. Dogs in a home environment typically feel more secure and remain more emotionally and behaviorally stable. Some rescues have experienced people who can help reform undesirable behaviors, making the dog more adoptable.

Case Study: Kip Had a Life in a Fishbowl

People who obtain a puppy and only allow the dog to become accustomed to the immediate family can end up with a dog whose life is the equivalent of life in a fishbowl. I suspected Kip, a Jack Russell terrier, had this issue. When I came to help with his training, I deduced his original owners never took him out of the house, leaving the dog insecure about people as well as the outside world. By a year old, Kip ended up in a rescue.

Kip was lucky he went to a no-kill shelter. He wouldn't have survived at many others, since he was extremely fearful most of the time he was there. When his adopters came to meet him, they waited in a room for the attendant to bring out the dog.

Kip rushed over to the mother of the family. She must have reminded him of his previous owner. He also felt comfortable with the younger son.

Kip was adopted and quickly found comfort through familiarity inside the house, the backyard, and with the immediate family members. However, he was afraid and very insecure on a walk and was also uncomfortable when anyone came over. Kip would avoid people he didn't know. Soon, defensive actions replaced avoidance because these intruders scared him, even though none of the visitors ever did anything adverse to the dog. Kip never learned to feel comfortable with more than a few family members, so when strangers came over, he would hide near a wall or a chair. Then, when people walked by, he began to rush and nip. Soon the nipping turned more consistently into biting of anyone who came in the house.

Having worked with a lot of fearful dogs, it is easy for me to picture that after Kip was brought home as a puppy, he never left the house except to go to a vet for shots. If people came over to his first home, no one worked to ease any fears Kip had about strangers. Perhaps Kip had already begun to bite when he was turned over to the rescue, or perhaps without any structured training, he'd become too much of a problematic dog. What I can say is I never witnessed Kip bite for any reason other than that he was afraid and insecure. Had his first owners taken Kip to a puppy class and followed up with a class during his adolescence, they'd have found he could be an enjoyable pet. Instead, Kip ended up in a shelter environment.

The lack of training and socialization in his original home made this dog a prime candidate to become all the more fearful and insecure in the rescue. This set him up for issues inside his new home. If his adoptive owners had not had the dedication to reform this dog, he'd have ended up in and out of shelters or rescues until his final journey to a kill shelter.

SHYNESS CREATED BY A MILL DOG ENVIRONMENT

For those of you not familiar with mill dogs, let me give you a quick rundown. Dogs in puppy mills are used to mass-produce puppies for pet shop sales or Internet sales. The parents of these puppies are kept in deplorable conditions where cages are stacked one on top of another. Mill dog breeders once inhumanely killed unwanted breeder dogs. Now many rescues work to save the dogs and re-home them. People adopting mill dogs often find them unsocialized and fearful.

If ever there was an experiment to see if a dog who was under-socialized and highly fearful could recover, the typical mill dog is that experiment. These dogs miss out on adequate socialization beginning in puppyhood and often continuing throughout a lot of the dog's life. Adding to these dogs' issues is that some are treated in ways to create more stress and fear, and some are physically abused. Most mill dogs are turned over to rescues at about seven years of age, when the dog's breeding ability is waning. I've helped several mill dogs recover from their highly fearful state and become like other normal dogs who had proper socialization. Given my success with mill dogs, I believe other dogs who were not adequately socialized when younger can make up for that lost opportunity with the right techniques.

Case Study: Otis and Albert

Otis, a poodle, and Albert, a long-haired Chihuahua, came from a mill dog breeding facility that was "cutting down" on its operation. The rescue suspected that the facility culled the worst fear biters. The other dogs who came in with Otis and Albert resolved their biting issues at foster homes. However, Otis's and Albert's issues were more pronounced, and they remained at the rescue for a year before I took them on as a project.

When these two four-year-olds arrived at my home, I had nothing to lose. If I failed to solve their extreme fear, including their fear-biting, since no one else had any success, my reputation wasn't under threat. I am glad to say that both dogs made a full recovery. I was surprised to discover that my idea of a mill dog's full recovery was different than some people's. I expected that the dog could learn to behave like any other dog that had adequate training and socialization. What I discovered is that too few people have this expectation, and instead of freeing the dog from fears, they merely house the dog in a less stressful environment. I can't imagine Otis enjoying his life if he didn't get to go for walks and car rides with his owner, trotting along behind her as if she'd raised him from a pup. Albert enjoys being a regular member of his family, although it is no secret that he is the canine favorite. What this all taught me was that even mill dogs, with the right training, can make a full recovery from fear.

When Otis and Albert arrived, they were afraid of just about everything. People were at the top of their fear list since the mill they came from was crueler to their dogs than some. Even breeding facilities that don't physically assault their dogs create a fearful environment for the dogs to live in. That generates dogs who are afraid of people and anything people try to do to them, as well as most other things in the world such as cars passing by on the street and household pets. You will hear more about these two dogs as I use them as examples of how to accomplish recovery with other dogs.

CREATING FEARFULNESS IN DOGS THROUGH ALPHA-HUMAN PROBLEMS

"Be your dog's alpha, be the leader of the pack!" has almost become a mantra with people who watched the *Dog Whisperer*. This philosophy gets conflicting results when people attempt this outdated approach to dog training.

Historically, dog training began with a punishment-based system. Typically the approach was reactive. When the dog did something wrong, you punished the dog so the dog would learn not to do that kind of behavior. The Monks of New Skete wrote their training books based on this system, and Cesar Millan used this approach in the show *Dog Whisperer*. I was also raised with this concept. About thirty years ago, if my golden retriever misbehaved, I'd call him to me, swat his behind, and tell him not to do that again. He actually learned this way what he could and couldn't do. After all, if a system never worked, no one would ever use it.

In the 1990s I got a Jack Russell terrier named Cookie for a pet. The first time I called her over for a reprimand was the last one. She came when I called that time, but after that when I called her for any reason, she would not come to me. Of course, I went to get her. After all, she needed to be shown who was boss. But, Cookie could read my anger and was not about to be caught. In the end, it was me who changed my ways, as this incident became the foundation of a different way to train dogs.

The moral of this story is that if you have been using reactive training and punitive techniques and getting away with it, there is a good chance you are reading this book because that isn't working with your dog. The good news is that over the years, I have accumulated techniques that can help you train your dog in a better way, even if you have a strong-willed dog who seems self-righteous like my Cookie.

Getting back to the human-alpha approach, there are several ways this can go wrong, especially with more fearful and insecure dogs. If you are dealing with a dog who is more submissive by nature, you will drive unwanted submissive behavior rather than resolve it with this approach. Another issue is that although your dog may learn to comply when you use disciplinary training, you can damage your relationship with the dog. Cookie taught me that with more independent and strong-willed dogs, the secret to compliance is to create a strong bond with them. A strong bond helps even a strong-willed and independent dog choose to comply. Physical punishment works against this kind of necessary bond.

The lack of disciplinary training doesn't mean that you end up with a spoiled dog or that the dog doesn't learn consequences for misbehavior. What it means is that you don't need to be harsh about your consequences. The root of your dog's ability to obey you willingly goes back to the dog's inbred behavior. Dogs like a strong leader and will more readily obey a strong leader. However, these days there is a lot of confusion about what is a strong leader to a dog. A lot of people think you need to be your dog's alpha or leader of the pack.

People have gathered the wrong idea about what kind of leader a dog really wants from shows such as *Dog Whisperer*. I will give Cesar Millan credit where credit is due. He has reformed a lot of dogs. But, I suspect very few of his television audience find any success trying to imitate him. That is in part because Cesar has learned how to effectively use outdated ways of correcting dog behavior. Much of his success comes from his talent in reading very subtle signals from dogs. He uses his ability to read a dog to effect changes in dog behavior, even with less-than-ideal techniques. I've worked for years on my talent in this area, and still feel he has an edge on me. Ironically, in more recent years, Cesar has diversified some of his techniques, incorporating less harsh ones. Unfortunately, too many people have been convinced that those leash jerks and alpha rolls are magic when it comes to solving dog behavior issues. I have a thriving consultation business from solving problems people created trying to play Dog Whisperer.

As for being your dog's alpha or the leader of the pack, or whatever you want to call it, the issue is that people misperceive how to achieve that role and what a dog really wants from us in that respect. Ironically, the kind of strong leader a dog likes to follow is a lot like the kind of leader we like to follow. And when was the last time someone you perceived as a strong leader needed to alpha roll you to gain your respect? Part of my goal in this book is to help people learn what Cookie taught me about how to change unwanted behavior through training, especially in highly fearful dogs, as well as help dogs resolve their fears.

Mishandling a Fearful Stage

Care Bear, a four-pound Yorkshire terrier, was very lovable. This ball of energy fluttered around the room to meet us, while we sat on the floor so as not to scare her. But, when her owner went to put on her leash and harness, everything changed. This leash-reactive dog had become so fearful about being on leash, she had learned to fear the leash itself.

Care Bear's leash reactivity began when she was seven months old. There are several ages when growing dogs can go through fear states, beginning at about eight weeks of age. The time when the dog encounters this state can vary with individuals. Care Bear reacted fearfully one day while out on a walk and began to bark at approaching people who scared her. When that didn't stop the people, she lunged and snapped to get rid of what she saw as a threat. This is not an uncommon way for a fearful dog to act, especially when on a leash.

Unfortunately, her owner took the wrong kind of action to solve this problem. Like too many people who religiously watched the *Dog Whisperer*, the owner tried to remedy Care Bear's problem with leash jerks and alpha rolls. That frightened Care Bear all the more, and she progressively became worse on her walks.

When I was called to consult on this issue, we began working with the dog inside the owner's house, since that should have been more neutral territory where the dog would more likely feel safe. At first, Care Bear seemed comfortable with us. But, when the owner tried to put on the harness and leash, the dog struggled and nipped fearfully at her owner. The entire time

Care Bear barked, at times in a frantic pitch. Once on the leash, I took charge of the dog. Care Bear lunged forward towards my assistant. When I used the leash to halt the dog, she turned and tried to bite me. The heart of the problem was that Care Bear didn't need to be corrected or punished for her fearful leash lunging, she needed training not to be fearful. By using the too harsh correction on the dog, the owner had created a problem that would take a lot more effort to correct.

CHAPTER 2
Socialization That Makes a Difference

Socializing can help many fearful dogs get past their issues. Conversely, the lack of socializing can create a fearful dog and can lead to behavior issues. Whether you have a regular dog, a reserved dog, or a shy dog, including those who are sensitive, socialization needs to be done correctly. Dog owners need to learn how much socialization the average dog needs and how best to obtain that level. Of course, dogs who are shy or reserved will need some extra help. For those dogs, a few extra techniques can help them over socialization hurdles.

WHAT IS ADEQUATE SOCIALIZATION?

Your dog's socialization and training can be compared to human socialization and training. With your children, you send them to school, where they begin their basic education as well as learn how to get along with other children. Although anyone can certainly homeschool a dog, dog classes offer an easy way of doing both training and socializing at critical ages. By taking your dog to a class as soon as the puppy's vaccinations are secure, you can have a great opportunity to begin your dog's socialization. But be choosy about that class. If you have a shyer puppy, you need to make sure you get an instructor who knows how to accommodate and improve that issue.

Some dog owners take their young dogs through a puppy class and then call that good enough. Both humans and dogs go through adolescence. For dogs, their adolescence begins around

25

four months old and can last until the dog is a year old. Just as our human-adolescent minds are rewiring, so are dogs'. And just as certainly as some humans experience turbulent times during this stage, so can some dogs. The best way to survive this stage is to enroll in an obedience class. In a good class that uses positive techniques, your dog will learn manners such as no longer being allowed the puppy behavior of jumping all over people.

The right structured training not only helps basic behavior, but offers socialization at a time the dog's socialization attitude is changing. During their adolescence, dogs work to find out their place in relation to the other members of their human and canine household. With some breeds, certain drives kick in. Dogs with guarding drives suddenly find themselves dealing with an urge to take action towards people and animals that make them uncertain. By training the dog at this critical stage, you can teach the dog to look to you for guidance rather than act in a way you won't approve of or that may cause danger to other people. Dogs with hunting drives often have that drive kick in during adolescence. I have known of Jack Russell terriers raised with a cat who, during adolescence, had their hunting drive kick in. Sometimes the cat doesn't survive that experience.

Some dogs go through adolescence with a minimum amount of training and socialization, settling down after a year of age. Just as young adults mature in their early twenties at different rates, dogs gain additional maturity through three years of age. And just as with people, some pass through this time with little consequence while others struggle with an identity crisis. With dogs, some will need additional counseling in the form of training to prevent the dog from trying to bully other dogs or people.

The amount of training dogs need at each stage of development can vary with individuals. Although some dogs may be fine with minimal training and socialization, more often dogs missing the needed training and socialization during different developmental stages can become unmanageable. If you keep up on the dog's training and socialization, you will find it easier to survive these stages. The easiest way to train and socialize is to enroll in a well-structured training class. People who neglect a dog's education, especially during adolescence, often give up the dog to a shelter. Sadly, all they needed to do was apply the correct training that includes socialization, as well as employ some patience.

Elmo Decided to Take On His Owner

When Elmo's owner Janet called me, she explained that she was having issues with her seven-month-old Airedale. He was biting her. He didn't attack aggressively, nor was he defending food or possession. What he was doing was treating her like a chew toy that he didn't respect. Respect was at the heart of this dog's problems. Elmo knew the word "no," but since he was an adolescent, he decided not to stop his behavior when he heard it. For Elmo to respond to this word, he needed to see Janet as a leader. The solution was to do leadership training and impulse control to regain compliance in this dog.

Elmo's issues were not unusual, especially for dogs who have more of a "take charge" attitude. Without training, during adolescence some dogs may decide to take charge in a household and only do what they want to do. With training, a dog can learn that since you are the leader, you will follow through and insure compliance.

Missing Training Opportunities

A lot of the suggested training development times, such as with puppies and during adolescence, are ideal times to shape good behavior in dogs. By doing the correct training at this time, you will expend less effort obtaining a well-behaved and socialized dog. However, if you missed that opportunity, there is still hope. One of the truly wonderful things about dogs is that no matter their age, they can learn to do just about anything.

COMPONENTS OF COMPLETE SOCIALIZATION

Some people are fooled about how much socialization dogs actually need. They may take a puppy to puppy class and feel their job is done. That marginal amount of socialization may work for a few dogs, but for many, especially dogs with a more sensitive, reserved, or shy nature, this is not adequate.

Dogs need to be socialized to different people, a variety of dogs, and to other animals including cats, other household pets, and livestock. The dog will need this kind of socialization both as a puppy and as an adolescent, and for some dogs, through three years of age. That means you will need to go beyond the offerings of a dog-training class to socially round out your dog.

As mentioned, some dogs are fine with less socialization. However, if you have a shy, reserved, or sensitive dog, you can expect that socialization will take more effort and the lessons may need to be refreshed from time to time. Shy dogs need a lot of exposure to different people and other dogs to learn to feel safe. Reserved dogs will need to meet a diverse number of people so they can assess who is okay and who is not okay. Sensitive dogs often need the same kind of socialization efforts as reserved and shy dogs. Soft dogs will need extra care during that socialization effort and will tend to saturate out the quickest during socialization efforts.

Sometimes it seems as though these three most problematic types of dogs assess other dogs and people by their differences rather than their similarities. Where people fall short when working to socialize their dog is that they expect since their puppy met eight or ten different dogs and owners in the puppy class, their dog will think all dogs and people are fine. Shy, sensitive, and reserved dogs often don't make that association. They understand that the puppies in that class are safe, but they won't automatically feel secure with new dogs they meet. In addition, these three most problematic types of dogs often associate security with a specific place. If you take the dog to a new place, the dog may feel insecure about that place with different noises and goings-on, making any canine or human introductions already off to a bad start. Therefore, you will benefit by exposing your dog to new places as well as making introductions to different dogs and people.

HOW TO TELL IF YOUR PUPPY NEEDS MORE SOCIALIZATION

Some breeds almost come with a tag that reads "extra socialization needed," while others seem fine with a bare minimum. If you have a herding breed, such as an Australian shepherd or a border collie, there is a good chance the dog will have a reserved nature and need extra socialization. Some of the working terriers, such as the Jack Russells, can have shyer individuals, increasing their needs. Often, retrievers can skate by with minimum socialization, but not always. I've also seen puppies who socially changed during adolescence. Owners need to watch for signals the dog needs help during the dog's first three years of life. If your dog begins to react with uncertainty in a new situation or with new people or other dogs, take the time to work to get the dog comfortable in those situations.

PREDICTING A DOG'S LONG-TERM SOCIAL APTITUDE

Although I've worked with a lot of dogs with issues, I can't always predict through the first three years of life how a dog is going to respond during different stages. I've had a highly socialized Jack Russell puppy become shy as an adolescent. This pup needed some extra help through that stage. I knew of a very social retriever mix who, after a year of age, started to have social difficulty with other dogs. She needed extra counseling to not be aggressive towards other dogs she suddenly saw as a threat.

29

Another dog who surprised me was a Boston terrier in one of my puppy classes. This Boston was extremely shy about all the other puppies. I expected this pup to need a lot of work, especially in the first year of life. Working with the dog's owner, we put in some extra effort to help the dog build confidence. Since the Boston was so fearful of all the other puppies, at first we didn't allow any of the other dogs to encounter this timid pup. Once the pup seemed more comfortable about hanging out in a "safe" corner of the room while watching the other pups interact, after class we allowed him to wander with a quieter puppy. Once those two became comfortable enough with each, they began to play in a more reserved manner. Soon, we felt we could add another more easygoing pup.

The Boston terrier made small steps each week towards feeling more confident. Then, something quite unexpected happened. This once-timid dog pulled at his collar, wanting to join in during the first playtime with the more rowdy dogs. When his owners let him go, he rough-and-tumbled with the best of them. As timid as he was in the beginning of the class, I expected him to be a shyer dog in general. But given the right opportunity, he came out of his shell.

CHECKLIST FOR A GOOD INSTRUCTOR AND A GOOD CLASS

Taking your dog to a training class is a great way to help train and socialize him, making the dog an enjoyable pet. However, that class needs to be a good one. Poor training classes can sometimes do more harm than good. Below are questions to ask an instructor to help evaluate a class. In addition to asking questions, consider watching one or two of the instructor's classes. Make sure the instructor is communicating well with the students and getting good results with the dogs.

Questions to Ask an Instructor

- Do you use positive techniques?
  If you know of a specific issue your dog has, such as acting
  stubborn when you ask the dog to sit, ask the instructor to
  tell you how he or she deals with this kind of issue. If the
  instructor resorts to shoving down the dog's back end, and
  then handing over a treat, I'd keep looking for a trainer
  with a better solution.

- Have you had experience with timid or reserved dogs?
  (Ask specifically about your breed.)
  If yes, ask them how they handle timid dogs. I like to see
  puppy classes have two playtimes to accommodate
  outgoing puppies and more timid dogs. This can be done
  by allowing the more rambunctious dogs playtime at the
  beginning of the class, and the timid ones playtime at the
  end. Sometimes a trainer owns a dog who is very good at
  helping with timid dogs and can do a little one-on-one time
  after class.

- How do you handle socializing the dog to people?
  The three most problematic types of dogs will need more
  than tons of people handling the dog; these dogs need
  correctly paced introductions. The instructor needs to give
  some examples of how he or she helped a more timid dog
  learn to feel more comfortable with strange people. That
  instructor needs to understand that quality interaction is
  much more important than quantity. The quality you look
  for is the instructor realizing the dog must relax with each
  encounter before moving on. The instructor needs to
  understand that typically the first few times the dog
  interacts with different people need to be limited so the
  dog doesn't become overwhelmed.

31

SOCIALIZATION GOALS OF A GOOD CLASS

One thing a good puppy class can provide is the opportunity for the puppy to be handled by adults and children. If no children are present in the puppy class, that kind of introduction needs to be secured elsewhere.

Not all puppy classes offer playtime. I prefer ones that do. However, the instructor needs to understand that inappropriate play needs to be discouraged, but not stopped. A good way to handle training for dogs that play incorrectly is to interrupt play that gets too intense, get the young dog to lower his energy level, and then allow the dog to again play. Although some dogs may need "time-outs" during the play learning process, the puppy also needs a chance to resume the activity to learn.

With an adolescent-level class, I like an instructor who works on teaching the young dog how to politely greet people and other dogs. In both cases, the dog should learn to wait for permission to approach. The dog also needs to learn that permission may not always be given. This teaches the dog correct human-to-dog social behavior.

For dogs who are adolescent or older, a great class to enroll in is one that works toward the American Kennel Club's Good Citizen Award. This award stresses good dog behavior, and classes that strive to teach dogs to earn that award turn out individuals who are a pleasure to own.

SOCIALIZING CHECKLIST

It is fine to pass puppies from person to person to be held. But, make sure the puppy has time to settle down and relax with the person holding the dog before handing the pup off to someone new. If you have a dog who is very timid, you need to work with people who have a calm and comforting demeanor to ensure success early on. Make sure the person agrees to hold the dog until the dog settles down, understanding that this may take a while. Sometimes this means holding the dog fifteen minutes or more.

Don't be in a rush to give the dog multiple experiences with people. Shyer dogs will need to conquer being held by strangers one at a time.

If you have a dog who seems fine being handed from person to person at first, then you notice the dog is no longer settling down with the new person, you have reached the dog's limit. Don't hand the dog to another person. Instead, give the dog whatever time it takes for him to again relax with the current person, then hand the dog back to the owner. However, don't hand the dog back while he is acting stressed, or the dog will regress in his fear.

Ideally, puppies, adolescents, and mature dogs are introduced to a variety of dogs and to men, women, and children who are different sizes, shapes, and ages. Although a puppy can have some leeway on manners, the dog can also begin to learn control. So don't hesitate to hold back a puppy who insists on plowing over a person with a greeting. Once the puppy gets more under control, the pup can greet that person. Of course, you may need to practice this several times before the pup can manage a more controlled greeting. With adolescent dogs and older, the goal is both positive introductions and correct manners.

USING TIME-TESTED TECHNIQUES FOR ERODING INSECURITY

Just as some dogs are shy, overly sensitive, or more reserved, so are some people. These kinds of people find ways avoid social situations. They don't attend a lot of social events, and if they get dragged to one, such as by a spouse, they often stand around looking more like a fixture than someone actively engaged in the group. Some people can live their lives this way, content to do so. However, sometimes this socially reclusive person's employer decides he or she is the perfect person to give a presentation for a product. A lot of people can find talking in front of a group intimidating. Just like a timid dog, shy, reserved, or overly sensitive people are more easily overwhelmed.

Although Toastmasters International was created to help people hone their speaking skills, the organization is littered with individuals who never in their lives wanted to get up in front of others and speak. They go to Toastmasters to conquer their fear. The organization is very skilled in helping socially shy people overcome their psychological barriers. Some of the same kinds of techniques can work for dogs who are socially challenged.

Ken Olson, Distinguished Toastmaster member/participant/speaker, has experience mentoring people who need to conquer their fear of public speaking. He has observed that it takes about six months for people to begin to get comfortable with speaking at the local Toastmasters club. In about a year, most are comfortable in the role of speaking.

What helps people get over this issue is taking small steps. The group is structured to prevent stalling out at any one point. The structure works for most people, starting with small challenges and working up to bigger ones. Challenges are necessary for change; however, the challenge needs to be at the right level for success. For example, people new to the group are not asked to take on the overwhelming task of speaking to the group as a whole. Instead, the newcomer helps with small tasks such as score keeping and timing of a speech. This gives the newcomer a chance to interact individually with people, which helps the person relax. After about a month, the person is asked to give an icebreaker speech where he or she talks for four minutes on any subject. The group helps support that person, working to get him or her through that first speech with success. Once that is accomplished, people are encouraged to do more speeches, taking things a little at a time. This formula works for many people, allowing most to conquer their fear of public speaking.

With dogs who are socially challenged, a good way to help is to think through and pace their socialization. The Toastmasters structure is a good one to follow. In both situations, you give the individual a chance to settle into a situation. Then you challenge the individual's sense of security, but do so at a tolerable pace. One way to do that is to take the dog to a new place and let him hang out and adjust to the goings-on. This gives the dog a chance to watch and observe while not feeling pressured. If there is some kind of activity you can do with the dog where the dog feels comfortable, similar to people new to Toastmasters being asked to keep time or score, try doing that. With your dog, that activity may be playing with you with a toy, or you may ask the dog to do a few commands for a treat. The message to the dog is to learn to feel relaxed at this place.

Once the dog feels comfortable in this new place, you can begin to ask for a few interactions. Make those interactions one-on-one introductions, but take your time. You need to ask for small steps at a time, ones that will bring success. And, just as that first speech for Toastmasters is a short one, you need to limit the amount of introductions you make with your dog. In general, you will be pushing the dog to gradually accept more and more, being careful not to do too much too fast.

Individuals Can Be Exceptions

Ken Olson did tell a story about one individual named Joe, where this time-tested structure didn't work. Like other people, Joe was allowed time to get used to his fellow Toastmasters at the weekly meetings. However, when it was time for Joe to give his icebreaker speech, things didn't go as it had for others before him. Joe walked up to the lectern, stood there for a minute, but couldn't seem to open his mouth. Then he turned and walked out of the room.

Members of the group tried to call Joe for over a month, but the calls went unanswered. Joe never returned to Toastmasters. Ken recalled that, looking back, Joe actually showed signs he wasn't ready to be pushed into this first speech. For Joe, the normal amount of time wasn't enough for him to feel secure. Unfortunately, his coach had a "throw them in and let them swim" attitude. While this idea worked for others over the years, people and dogs are individuals. There is no guarantee that the same time frame works for all.

The moral to Joe's story is, even if you are working a dog through social shyness using a time-tested formula, you need to be sure the animal is able to go at that pace. Just because it worked for all the other dogs doesn't mean simply going through the steps is all you need to do. You need to make sure the dog is ready to move from one step to another, even if it means taking more time than the others. You may also find you need to tweak your technique for a specific dog.

SHY OR ABUSED?

An incident about twenty years ago did a lot to educate me about working with extremely shy dogs. We had our terrier Alexis at a dog show, and my daughter was working to introduce her to a stranger. My daughter asked the man to greet the dog. When this large man bent to pet Alexis, the dog flailed, emitting the equivalent of a canine scream. One person at the show assumed the issue was that Alexis had been abused by a man and stated she had a rescue she felt had the same problem. I knew Alexis had never been abused by anyone, man or woman.

I've learned a lot since we owned Alexis and can easily see several mistakes in that introduction. I've often observed that many shyer dogs are easily intimidated by large men. Although Alexis was raised in a family with two six-foot-tall men who had a more powerful demeanor, being comfortable with family members does not socialize a dog to strangers. Making matters worse was that Alexis was somewhat stressed, since this was one of her first dog shows. Before you work on introducing a shy dog, that dog needs to feel calm. Some dogs will need several visits to a dog show or other environment to calm down.

Another issue was that the introduction was done incorrectly. This man was leaning over the dog as he reached towards the top of her head. Looming over a dog is a very intimidating way to greet a fearful dog. A better way to do this would be to have the man talk with my daughter until the dog relaxed, then have the man get down to Alexis's level and let the dog move towards him, not the other way around. Giving a treat can help a dog move forward. If Alexis failed to relax after about fifteen minutes, it would be better not to ask the dog to greet this person.

A lot of people mistake dogs who are highly fearful as being victims of abuse. I've worked with dogs who were abused and find the dog quickly recovers with the right opportunity, filling me with admiration of the dog's willingness to forgive and forget human trespasses. However, I have also worked with dogs who have a very fearful nature and have found it takes much longer to solve fear issues in this kind of dog than in a dog who was abused.

SOCIAL EXPECTATION OF DOGS

With regular dogs, the sooner you begin socializing the dog, the easier the task will be. It is best to keep up the work until the dog is three years old and socially mature. With guarding breeds, such as Rottweilers and German shepherds, you will need to work extra hard during their adolescence. This is when the dog's guarding drive kicks in. Your work will be focused on teaching the dog what not to react to. If you are dealing with shy, reserved, or sensitive dogs (the problematic three), don't be

37

surprised to find your dog needs extra effort through three years of age.

With the three problematic types of dogs, the more exposure to different people and different situations, the more information the dog has to assess that things are okay. You need to begin early, and keep up the work. Anything that causes the dog to regress needs to be worked through as soon as possible. Always work to end on a positive note.

With soft and sensitive dogs, you can have extra challenges when working to socialize them. If the dog is noise sensitive, you need to make sure he doesn't become insecure because of a noise before you allow any human or dog introductions. If you own a soft dog, you will find yourself trying to manage the people wanting to meet your dog. People coming up to a soft dog will upset the dog if they make direct eye contact. The dog may also become unnerved if people approach too directly. Soft dogs prefer someone coming up slowly and walking indirectly towards them while glancing towards the ground. With the soft dog, you need to make sure you never scold the dog. Instead, look for behaviors you can reward. An excited or high-pitched voice may not work for the fearful or soft dog. Many soft dogs prefer a calm, reassuring tone.

CASE STUDIES

Merlin

Most golden retrievers don't need to learn to *want* to greet people, they need to learn *how* to greet people politely rather than jump all over them. Merlin didn't seem to understand that rule. At two years of age, he was very afraid of people. At the heart of Merlin's problems was that he was a more timid dog who had grown up in a home where he had too much isolation. Although Merlin was not at all aggressive towards people he didn't know, he would slink away into corners to hide anytime someone came over to the house. If people tried to approach him, he'd flee. Adding to Merlin's issues were two things: First, he only encountered people in his home and few people came over to the home in his first two years, and second, nothing was done to let Merlin know he really didn't need to be so afraid.

When Merlin was two years old, Judy moved to town. With more people coming by the house, she realized she had to resolve Merlin's terror of strangers. Judy came up with a rather clever idea. Since the summer had just begun and she had rented a booth at a farmers' market, she decided to take Merlin with her each day. She created a secluded area in the booth where Merlin could stay in a crate, where he felt safe. There, he had a chance to adjust to the sight of people milling around. Every so often, Judy would go over and offer a treat to Merlin. At first he would not take the treat, so Judy left it right in front of the dog and walked off. Soon she noticed he'd eat the treat she left. As Merlin began to relax about his environment, he started to accept a treat directly from Judy. Since the dog had learned to relax about that one area, Judy moved his crate a little closer to the foot traffic. She did this incrementally, making sure at each stage Merlin relaxed enough to directly eat a treat from her.

By the end of the month, Merlin was ready to take on more of a challenge, so Judy built him a three-sided barrier near the center of her booth for him to stay inside instead of a crate. This offered Merlin more exposure while still giving the dog a sense of some seclusion. Each week, Judy removed a part of the three-sided barrier. By the end of the second month, Merlin felt comfortable lying near the center of the booth area with no barriers for seclusion.

Now it was time for Judy to teach Merlin to lie closer to the foot traffic, without any crate or barrier to hide in. Judy took her time moving Merlin closer and closer. After each move, she'd check to see if Merlin had relaxed by offering a treat. When he calmly accepted a treat, he was ready to move closer.

Once Merlin learned to relax about people going by, it was time to let folks greet her dog. Judy began this process by letting a stranger drop a treat in front of him. Soon, Judy was able to let a few more calm and friendly people lower to the dog's level to greet him. Once Merlin accepted that, she let people give him a treat then pet him under his chin. She never allowed any of the greeters to lean over him to greet him. By the end of the season, Merlin was more secure about people approaching him and greeting him.

Analyzing What Worked

Judy told me that when she picked up Merlin from the breeder, she noticed that the pup held back when the other puppies bounded forward to greet people. This puppy's more timid tendencies along with a lack of socialization created a dog who was very fearful of strangers. Judy needed to do the right things to help socialize this dog. Following is what was important and why.

The crate helped the dog feel secure. Of course, it is important that the dog already feels secure inside a crate. Judy had done that part before she took Merlin to the farmers' market.

At first Judy didn't allow any interactions with people. Merlin was already uncertain enough being in that crate with all those people coming by. That was evident, since he didn't want to eat a treat at first. Dogs who are too nervous will often turn down a treat. If Judy had tried to bring people near the crate for Merlin to meet before he was secure enough to eat a treat, he may have lost his sense of security inside the crate. He may also have begun to get apprehensive the whole time he was at the farmers' market, worrying about when someone was going to approach him in an area where he may have felt trapped.

Once Merlin became secure in the crate while people milled around, Judy changed to a crate-like enclosure that allowed her to gradually remove the sides. This gave Merlin time to adjust little by little to being more in the open while people walked about in a similar fashion as they had before.

Dropping or offering a treat for Merlin to eat every so often not only gave him a positive association with his new situation, it gave Judy a chance to know when he was beginning to calm down about the change. If he readily ate the treat, he was ready to move to the next stage. If he was hesitant or unwilling to eat the treat, he needed more time.

Judy was wise not to try to introduce people during the time she worked to get Merlin used to lying in the open while people milled around. He had shown too much fear about people coming to her home to rush this part of the dog's training. She needed to allow him extra time to feel more secure before people were introduced.

Once Merlin relaxed about lying in the center of the booth while people walked around, he was ready to move closer to people. Again, Judy was clever to take things at his pace. When she did let him begin to interact with people he didn't know, she helped him out by not allowing contact at first. All she asked of the dog was to accept a treat from strangers. Once he realized that people coming up to him was a good thing, he was ready to try a greeting. By selecting the right kind of people, those with a calmer, less threatening demeanor, she gave Merlin a better chance at success. Success early on is very important. Also, by having people crouch to his level and touch him under his chin or on his chest, she made sure he would more likely accept that first contact. Dogs who are insecure do well with strokes under their chin rather than pets on top of their head.

Abby

I adopted Abby when she was three years old. This dog was a reserved dog. She had exposure to a limited amount of people; however, she had met a lot of different dogs through her first owner. Abby was great with other dogs, but she held back with

41

people she didn't know, and was very uncertain about children. Once she got to know a person, she was very friendly with that individual. I introduced her to a few neighbor children to get her used to kids. Once she got to know them, she'd go right over to them for a pet when they came to visit.

As with most reserved dogs, as well as shy dogs and sensitive dogs, only introducing a few children to the dog is not adequate. To help Abby get more accepting of children she didn't know, I took her to a library where I was giving a talk on dog behaviors. During my talk, Abby stayed in a crate at the front of the room. Afterwards, a few kids wanted to come up and meet my dog. I let Abby out and watched to see how she reacted to the kids. Of course, I showed the kids how to greet her the right way by first petting her chest. Abby seemed quite comfortable. I figured she had time to get used to them while in the crate, and that helped a lot.

A week later while walking out on a trail, I came across a group of children. Since the kids were wanting to pet dogs, I worked to introduce them to another dog I was socializing. I noticed Abby joined right in, walking over to the kids for pets as if she didn't know she was a reserved dog. It is important to note that keeping up this kind of socialization makes a difference. If Abby didn't have a chance to again greet children for months, her positive experience may have waned. Since she had an opportunity to greet kids so soon after a positive experience, she made nice progress.

CHAPTER 3

House-Training Challenges in Rescues and Fearful Dogs

Are rescue dogs more difficult to house-train? Can fearfulness in a dog create additional house-training challenges? How old is too old to house train a dog? What causes a house-trained dog to regress? These are only a few of the questions from people who are having house-training issues. The good news is that barring any medical conditions, dogs can be successfully house-trained at any age. That being said, there are some dogs who are more prone to house-training problems, including more fearful dogs.

DOING THINGS RIGHT FROM THE BEGINNING

At a presentation I did, a woman came to my talk for one specific problem. Her year-old dog, which she'd acquired as a puppy, was still not house-trained. It didn't take me long to figure out where things had gone wrong. The elderly woman was using the same approach that had worked for her in the past, but can fail for too many dogs. What I have found is that dogs who have some of the traits discussed in chapter one are often prime candidates for failing house training when people employ punitive training techniques. In this case, when the dog had an accident, the woman took the dog to the issue on the carpet, shoved the dog's nose into the mess, swatted the dog's back end, then put the dog outside. Using punishment to house-train a dog can fail more often than work. Sometimes punishment can create other issues such as submissive peeing. These days, we know better ways to achieve success.

HOW TO TRAIN A YOUNG DOG

House training, in essence, is simple. A dog has a natural instinct to keep his den clean. If you teach the dog your entire house is a den, you will find success house training your dog. There are, of course, a few ground rules. First, puppies are not old enough to comprehend an area as large as your entire house as a den. They need to start small and work up to a bigger area. And second, a young dog can't hold things all day. I've provided a table to help you get an estimate as to what you can expect.

Realizing that the puppy can't hold things for the eight to nine hours while you are at work doesn't solve how to deal with this issue. If you need to house-train a dog but are not home during the day, you will need to accommodate the dog until the dog matures enough to hold things until you get home. Although some people can arrange for a neighbor to come inside the house to let the young dog out, for others, this isn't possible. There are some other options to help.

To begin the house training, set up a playpen or use a room you can puppy-proof. You may also use a doggy RV setup as described below. Although the eventual goal is to teach your dog that the entire house is the equivalent of a den, as mentioned, most young dogs are not mentally mature enough to understand that an area as large as your house is considered a den, so you need to start with a small area. As the dog matures physically and mentally, you can expand that area. Until that time, you will find success training your dog if you limit the area the dog can roam and if you are around to let the dog out before he eliminates in the house.

If you can't be around to let the dog out when the dog needs to go, consider arranging an indoor toilet. I know some people may panic at this idea. After all, one certainly would like to set up the right habit from the beginning. But for many people, this may not be practical. What can work is to confine the dog in an area where you can offer a clean space and a restroom area. This kind of arrangement begins the process of teaching the dog that some areas are for living in and some are for answering the call of nature. Once the dog is older, you can change the rules so the dog understands the entire house is the clean "den" area and the outside is the "answer the call of nature" area.

Many people use puppy pads to line the area where their dog is confined during the day. There are a few rules you need to follow with puppy pads. With a very young dog, a lot of puppy pads all over a small room is fine. However, you also need to establish a sleeping or den area when you use puppy pads. That way the young dog can learn from the beginning that sleeping areas are separate from potty areas. Once the puppy shows a pattern of eliminating in one area, remove the puppy pads from the unused areas so the dog learns to keep the business in one place. If the dog misses the puppy pad, be sure to clean up that spot.

As the dog matures physically, he can hold things the entire day, and you can expand the "den" area to include the entire house. Both physical ability and the mental maturity to understand that the entire house is a den to be kept clean will vary with individuals and breeds. In general, northern breeds like the husky seem to grasp the "den" concept quite early. Many smaller breeds may take several months to completely get the "where to go and where not to go" concept. Although this may try your patience, if the dog just isn't figuring things out, make sure you are using the right techniques. If you are, you may be dealing with a young dog who is slower to mature mentally and "get" this concept.

Physical maturity is also an issue for some dogs. Some dogs also are slower at achieving urinary control. Even though they begin to eliminate outside, they may stop in the middle of playing with an almost uncontrollable urge. Don't yell at the dog, but try to coax the dog outside, even if he gets some urine on the carpet. Leave the puppy out while you thoroughly clean the area, then let the dog back in. This can help teach the dog both mentally and physically to transfer this outside. If you are dealing with this kind of bladder control challenge, you will need patience. It can take a few months for the dog to develop the ability to hold things when playing.

When you are home on the weekend, don't hesitate to take the puppy outside to use the facilities. This can help progress the house-training goal you want to reach once the young dog is old enough to wait inside the home while you are away at work.

Know Your Dog's Limitations

Most dogs adhere to the table below as far as age and ability to hold things.

Dog Age	Time
2 months	2 hours
3 months	4 hours
4 months	5 hours
6 months	7 hours
7 months	8 hours

Cleaning Up Accidents the Right Way

Use an enzymatic cleaning solution, such as Nature's Miracle, to help eliminate the smell if there are accidents in any inappropriate areas. Be aware that things like vinegar may only partially mask the odor.

DOES GOING INSIDE SABOTAGE GOING OUTSIDE?

I know some people who are adamant about working to make sure the dog never goes inside the house. They believe that this sets up the strongest possible commitment in a dog for future reference. Only letting a dog go outside does have an advantage; however, for many people this is not attainable.

If you can't prevent accidents inside the house, or if you obtain a rescue who was never house-trained, such as many mill dog rescues, don't worry. I've seen success obtained with dogs who began their house training at any age. One older mill dog rescue, a German shepherd, never seemed to need to be house-trained. She'd struggled to hold things until she could get outside (she'd lived her life in an outside pen before going to a rescue). The dog appeared to have a very strong "den" instinct.

What will sabotage house-training efforts the most are emotional issues (discussed in detail in the next chapter) and when people use punitive training techniques. I understand why people use rubbing a dog's nose into its mess or punishing a dog for accidents; I grew up learning those techniques. But, like I said, with too many dogs, this can actually create a more resistant problem, which was what happened to the woman who came to my dog talk. Better ways to approach house training include arranging to have the dog outside at the times he is more likely to need to eliminate and to reward the dog when he has success.

Best Times to Take Your Dog Out

After exercise or playing

After eating

After waking up

If the dog hasn't been out for a while

If the dog begins to sniff around the floor

Potty Facts

Many people wonder just how long a mature dog can "hold" things. Dogs will often hold things overnight between twelve and fourteen hours. During the day, they can endure similar marathons as long as they are not too active. Since dogs tend to be more active during the day, it is reasonable to expect them to need to answer the call more often. That being said, dogs can be trained to go on cue. Some people train this when they take the dog outside to answer the call. They attach a command to the event such as "get busy" or "go potty."

HOW LONG TO STAY OUTSIDE

Have you ever put a dog outside, let him in, then within half an hour found a mess on the floor? This is not uncommon. One way to avoid this is to use a leash and spend some time outside when first working to house-train a dog. When you snap a leash on the dog and escort him outside, you can be right there to reward the dog for doing his business where you want him to do his business. Although some people have had success by simply putting the dog out, with more fearful and less secure dogs, escorting the dog outside on a leash and walking until the dog does his business, along with giving a reward, brings you quicker success.

Some people are surprised how long it can take when first working with a dog to get the dog to understand he needs to go outside. Some dogs will get distracted and begin to play. That is why having the dog on a leash helps. The leash can keep the dog more on task, especially if you walk back and forth in the same area. I prefer walking the dog as far away from the house as practical. This establishes a good protocol of isolating the event from your den/house. As to how long this may take, the first time can take a while. Some dogs may take half an hour or more. On the bright side, since you are walking the dog on a leash, the movement will help stimulate the dog to need to go sooner.

House-Training Tips

- To optimize success, work to take the dog out at an opportune time for the dog's age and needs as shown in the two tables.

- If the dog has success, wait until he is completely done eliminating before praising him. If you praise too soon, you can interrupt the dog before he is done, and the dog may not get his entire business concluded.

- When giving a treat for eliminating in the right place, use a "high-value" treat. My favorite high-value treat is a small piece of meat. I keep little chunks in the freezer, all ready to go. Use this high-value treat exclusively for house training.

- Once the dog begins to cue you to go outside, allow the dog to go outside without you. But, make sure the dog gets all of his business done before letting him back inside. When the dog asks to come back inside, reward with a different treat at the door, one with less value.

- Quit feeding treats at the door after the dog has a few success, but keep up the praise intermittently for a while longer.

Reprimands and Emotions Work against Success

With some dogs, you may find it takes time to achieve success. Although it is tempting to use reprimands or a stern tone with the dog, resist this impulse. Drawing attention to this issue by being angry or making comments to the dog will work against success. Just clean things up and employ patience. If you have a dog who began to have success but then regressed, you will find more information on how to deal with that in the next chapter.

Another unintended problem is showing disapproval when a dog has an accident. Even if you have worked diligently on house training and now have an accident to clean, keep an even demeanor. Don't show disapproval, and don't use a chirpy "it's okay" tone. Both can be stressful to a dog, and stress works against success in the long run. Soft dogs are especially susceptible to becoming stressed about house training if you show disapproval. The less stressed the dog feels about the house-training process, the sooner you will achieve success.

USING CRATES FOR HOUSE TRAINING

Some people worry that using crates is cruel. That is only true if they are used incorrectly. Incorrect uses include confining a dog to a crate excessively and using a crate for punishment. When used correctly, crates can become an invaluable tool for house-training success along with other behavioral issues. Many dogs find the crate a place of comfort.

There are a lot of ways to crate-train a dog. When choosing a technique, make sure you use a positive one. One of my favorites is to coax the dog inside the crate with a treat. Select a treat the dog needs some time to eat. The first time I do this, I close the door once the dog is inside and allow him to enjoy the treat. Just before the dog finishes the treat, I quietly open the door. I like to stay near the crate while the dog is inside, so he associates being in the crate with me being nearby.

The next time I do this, I leave the dog inside the crate for a short time after he finishes the treat. If the dog paws or fusses, I sit quietly beside the crate and wait until he quiets down. As soon as the dog is quiet, I put a small, quickly eatable treat inside to reward him for settling down, then open the door.

When working to extend the dog's time in the crate, you may want to have that crate nearby while you watch television. If the dog seems content inside the crate, occasionally walk off and come back. Once the dog seems fine with your leaving, try leaving the dog for longer periods of time. It is a good idea to give the dog a chew item to occupy him during the first fifteen minutes to half an hour the first few times you do this.

One of the ways crates help with house training is that crates are confining, and lower activity reduces the urge to eliminate in a dog. Conversely, more activity creates a greater need to go in a dog. You may have noticed that even younger dogs seem to be able to stay all night in a crate without an accident, but need to go outside more often during the day. You may have also noticed that many dogs seem to need to answer the call of nature soon after you begin a walk. That is one of the reasons to leash and walk the dog in the backyard when working to train a dog where to go. By keeping the dog moving, you hasten the dog's need to answer the call of nature.

Dealing with Accidents in the Crate

Sometimes a dog can have an accident in the crate. Time is of the essence when it comes to cleaning up any messes in a crate. If you have some kind of crate pad, it will need to be thoroughly cleaned to eliminate any traces of odor. If the dog has a lot of accidents, you may want to try using inexpensive towels, buying enough to have several to switch out before needing to launder them. If the dog has an accident, immediately remove the towel. Use cleaner on any area of the crate floor that was affected, then replace the towel with a new one. Some dogs seem to require patience for a few weeks before they learn to keep their crate clean. Other dogs have a chronic issue and need to be retrained to keep their crate clean.

Why Some Dogs Won't Keep a Crate Clean

It has been recommended in the past to make sure the crate is not too large for a dog, especially a young dog. The idea is that if the dog is in too large of a crate, the dog can learn to eliminate in one part of the crate and sleep nearby. There can be a flaw in this approach. If a dog has an accident and the crate is so small the dog is forced to lay in the elimination, that can sabotage the dog's natural sense not to eliminate in a sleeping area or a den. I feel the ideal size is one that isn't so big as to invite the dog to use one corner as a bathroom, yet not too small so the dog is forced to lay in any eliminations.

Many mill dogs have learned to live with their elimination in a crate or cage. This often occurs because cages are stacked one on top of the other. Dogs in the top crate live in filth until they step on feces, sending it on that long path through other occupied cages to the area underneath the bottom cage.

With some dogs, you may not know what caused them to sleep in filth, just that they simply don't seem to get the idea that they shouldn't sleep in messes. When I am confronted with a dog who doesn't understand the concept of keeping the sleeping area clean, whether the dog is a mill dog or one who didn't learn to keep a crate clean, I use a similar approach to solving the problem. I create the equivalent of a doggy RV.

Creating a Doggy RV

My experience in creating a doggy RV is with small dogs. At the expense of sounding biased, they typically have a lot more house-training issues. If you are working with a medium-size or large dog, you will need a small pen or confinement area inside your home. With small dogs, obtain a very large dog crate for the RV part. Inside the doggy RV, put a restroom area and a sleeping area in a contained area, much like a human RV. A water dish can be clipped on the side.

For your doggy RV restroom, you can use a small box that contains material for the dog to eliminate on. Just be sure that if you have a male dog, the sides of the box are high enough to catch any urine when the dog lifts a leg to pee. Some people use a small crate inside the RV for the potty area. Often the crate can be disassembled, since all you need is the lower half of the crate for the potty area.

There are several things you can put in the potty area. Puppy litter is available to help keep down odor. This greenish pelleted substrate can be found at most pet supply stores. I prefer to use dirt from the outside, since that is where I hope to have the dog eventually learn to go.

Once the dog is set up in this RV, I find many of them quickly learn to use the restroom area and keep their sleeping area clean. There are a few aids you can use for more resistant dogs. Early on, put a sample of the dog's feces in the potty area as an example. If the dog eliminates in the sleeping area, clean it up immediately. For chronic cases, you can employ a stack of towels for the sleeping area so you can easily get rid of any accidents. Be sure to use an enzymatic cleaner on any soiled areas outside the potty area. If, after a week, the dog is still consistently eliminating in the sleeping area, elevate the bed. I've seen a hammock type of dog bed for sale that is a few inches high. Elevated beds are more challenging to eliminate on. Keep the dog in this arrangement until he learns to keep the sleeping area clean for at least a month.

Transitioning to a Regular Crate
Once the dog has success keeping the sleeping area of the RV crate clean for an extended period of time, you can transition into a regular crate. However, if you had to elevate the sleeping

area, be sure to let the dog get used to sleeping in a non-elevated bed successfully before trying a regular crate.

Ideally, choose a time when you are going to be home for a few days. Put the dog in the crate, but take the dog outside often. Reward the dog for any and all eliminations done outside. If the dog does have an accident inside the crate, clean it up completely, eliminating any odors. Immediately replace the bedding. You may want to use that stack of towels to help. Be patient. I've seen it take a few months at this stage to achieve complete success.

If the dog seems intermittent about eliminating in the crate, even though you take him outside, try a hammock type of bed in the crate. These beds typically have PVC pipe on the perimeter, but sag in the middle. Lying in the center of the bed is comfortable, but trying to walk around a lot is not. That inability to walk around can discourage the dog from trying to eliminate in the bed. If you find the dog is regressing with house training in the regular crate, go back to the doggy RV and don't try again until the dog shows complete success for two or three months.

Otis and Albert's RV

Otis and Albert were mill dog rescues who got a "get out of jail free" card because both of them had rather significant fear-biting issues. I decided to foster them after they had spent a year at their rescue and made no improvement with their defensive biting. When they arrived at my home, both of these four-year-old dogs had never had the opportunity to go to the bathroom outside of a crate or kennel.

The first thing I did was set up a doggy RV like I described above. I chose to use dirt in the restroom area. I also took the precaution of lining the sides of the large wire RV crate with plastic. This turned out to be a good decision because Albert loved to mark everything. When I say "loved" what I mean is that I had never seen a dog take such glee in hiking his leg on any and every surface. Otis was quite the opposite. He never in his life hiked his leg, even though both dogs were used for breeding.

The RV training went quite well with both dogs. Both got the idea rather quickly to use the facility. However, though Albert used the restroom area of his RV, he also marked different sides of the wire RV crate. It is important to understand that male marking is a separate issue from regular house training. You will find that subject covered in more detail later in this chapter.

Even though both dogs sharing the same RV worked out fine as far as house training, it didn't work out for dealing with their fear and insecurity issues. To achieve success with that training, I found I had to separate them into individual crates located in different rooms. Since they'd both gotten the idea of keeping their sleeping area clean at that time, I put each in a regular crate rather than in an RV crate. Albert quickly adjusted to doing his business outside, except for occasionally marking the corners of his crate. That issue was eventually solved using methods for male marking.

Otis had more issues. It took him a long time not to occasionally have an accident inside his crate. Some mornings he'd bark for me to let him out if he felt I was running a little later than he'd like. Then the next morning, he wouldn't bark but would leave a deposit near the front of the cage. I kept it clean and didn't reprimand him about the issue. After a few months of intermittent problems, he finally got the idea and became reliable. The only relapse Otis had was after he'd been adopted. After a few weeks at his new home, a friend's dog came to visit. After the dog left, Otis became quite upset, barking at the front door. He also left a mess there. The new owner cleaned it up, and the problem didn't repeat. Had she reprimanded or punished Otis, she could have created a more long-term issue.

In general, using reprimands and punishment for fearful and more insecure dogs can result in the dog turning house training into an emotional issue. When this happens, the house-training problem can become chronic. That type of problem is discussed more in the next chapter.

ACCLIMATING A RESCUE TO YOUR HOME

When I adopted Abby, a three-year-old Australian shepherd, I was delighted that she was already house-trained. Still, I took precautions and took her outside several times. I figured by my taking her outside, she'd have a lot of opportunity to not only go if she needed, but learn which door she needed to ask at to go outside. Although this approach can work with a lot of dogs, it didn't work for Abby. Half an hour after she came back inside, she left a pile on my carpet. The incident did teach me other ways of helping acclimate new dogs to a home.

Dogs new to a home are more likely to feel somewhat stressed. That is why they often need to use the facility at unusual times even though mature dogs can typically hold things for a long time. What I later discovered was that Abby wasn't particularly used to holding things. She was used to a doggy door. She may have gone to the door just before her accident, and I hadn't noticed. Or she may have looked for a doggy door and not found one.

A better way to approach acclimating a dog to your home is to take the dog outside fairly soon after he arrives home. This may be challenging if you have kids or others wanting to lavish the dog with love, but you need to ask for patience from other family members. Go outside with the dog on a leash and walk around much like you would with a young dog. Be ready to reward any successes with a treat. If you don't have success, then go and greet the family and relax for about an hour. But keep the dog nearby and watch him. After the dog seems to settle down a little about being in a new home, again take the dog outside, only this time, go for at least a half-hour walk. If the dog has success, reward him with quiet praise and give him a treat. If the dog doesn't have success, again keep an eye on the dog while in your house. After your evening meal, again take the dog outside. Be sure to take the dog outside before bedtime.

Even with the best strategies, you might end up with an accident in the house. For Abby, this only happened the first day. What helped this issue to resolve quickly was that I didn't fuss or scold her. I quietly cleaned up the mess, placing the pile outside in the area she needed to use. I also thoroughly cleaned the area. If you are having issues after the first day, you may try using a crate to confine the dog, or keep the dog tied nearby you. If you use a crate, don't isolate the dog, but keep the crate near where people will be around. It is very important not to have crates symbolize isolation to a dog, especially with a new arrival.

DOGS WHO SNEAK DOWN THE HALL

Some dogs learn that eliminating in the main part of the house is off-limits, but for whatever reason, the dog figures a more isolated area is fine. These dogs will sneak off to a bedroom or quiet area to relieve themselves. Sometimes dogs go under tables or beds. If this is your problem, you need to do some more work to complete your house training.

The first thing to do is to block off those areas, and be fairly vigilant about making sure the dog learns to go outside to use the facilities in the main part of your house. Once the dog shows success in the main part of the house, only let the dog have access to the rest of the house when you can watch him. If you see the dog heading down the hall or towards a favorite elimination area, call the dog to you and take him outside. Make sure the dog does his business before coming in, and be sure to praise the dog for the right action. Expect to put in some work to break the dog's habit of regarding more isolated areas as a restroom.

Albert Sneaked Down the Hall

When Albert was first learning not to go inside my house, I used a baby gate to keep him in the living room and kitchen area to teach him the "house is a den" concept. After he began to have success going outside, I removed the baby gate. However, every so often I'd find a mess in a back bedroom. To counter this, I became diligent about watching him. If I saw him begin to wander down the hall, I'd call him to me and put him outside. By my interrupting his attempts to go inside, and making sure he followed up by doing his business outside, he learned that house training wasn't just about privacy in an isolated area, but about going entirely outside the house.

CASE STUDIES OF RESISTANT DOGS

Although I've strongly recommended leashing a dog and walking outside to get the dog to do his business, for some dogs this may not work as well as it does for others. So it was for Kelly, who owned Boston terriers, a breed she became hooked on after owning Hoosier. While Hoosier wasn't the first dog she'd house-trained, he certainly was the most challenging. Even though she'd put him outside for a while, after he came back inside, he'd go to the bottom of the stairs and relieve himself. To break this unwanted habit, Kelly put Hoosier on a leash and tied the leash to her belt loop. If Hoosier tried to wander off, Kelly would escort him outside to do his business. Although Hoosier's house training took time and commitment, once he got the idea, he became very reliable.

By the time Kelly got her second Boston, Toby, she was wise to the sneaking-off trick and got right to work preventing this unwanted behavior by tethering the dog. She also worked to encourage the right way to do things with rewards. The "rewarding the dog outside for the correct behavior" was key since these boys had the attitude that no matter how long they were outside, they could hold it until they got back in the house. Kelly knew she could never reprimand any unwanted behaviors, especially since both dogs were very sensitive. To Kelly, it seemed that once that little lightbulb went off in the dog's head and the dog realized what he was suppose to do, the dog became reliable.

The Problem with Iggys

Iggys, or Italian greyhounds, can be somewhat challenging when it comes to house training. Other breeds, such as Chinese cresteds, can also have similar issues. Behind the problem is the fact that these dogs don't like to go outside if there are any kinds of adverse weather conditions. Instead, they will do their business inside on rainy or cold days. Unfortunately, sometimes people try to punish the dog for this issue. Since these dogs are sensitive to reprimands, punishment can create a very insecure dog or even fearful dog while making the house-training problem worse.

When Kim Gillespe took on her first Iggy, Boomer, she inherited a problem created by the previous owner. That owner had generated a fearful situation with the dog by using punishment for house-training mistakes. Not only did this result in the dog not succeeding with house training, but the dog became too afraid to do his business anytime people were around. This created a challenge for Kim when it came to taking the dog outside to try to reward the dog for successful eliminations.

Kim came up with a rather clever idea to solve this problem. She used a clicker to get the dog to associate the sound of a clicker with a treat. Then, she scheduled in a long period of time on a nice day. She went outside and walked the dog around.

Anytime the dog did any motions that indicated the need to answer the call, Kim clicked and treated. Though it took hours, the dog finally found the courage to go to the bathroom when Kim was around. This helped her train the dog the right way.

Jeff and Tater

Jeff had dogs all of his life. After losing one of his favorite old dogs, he decided to get the next dog from a rescue. His five-month-old terrier mix was named Tater. The dog was supposed to be house-trained, but Tater was not going outside to do his business. Jeff, being in his early fifties, had always house-trained dogs by pushing the dog's nose in the mess, scolding, and putting the dog outside. He tried this on Tater, but had no success. In fact, the dog's issues were seeming to get worse because Tater was sensitive to reprimands.

I had a discussion with Jeff about abandoning the old-fashioned techniques and using positive techniques instead. He agreed to give it a try. When I checked with him a few days later, Jeff said things were improving a little, and he'd keep up rewarding the dog for success rather than punishing mistakes. It only took a few weeks and things turned around for Tater. Jeff chuckled as he told me that his daughter had taken Tater out when the dog asked to go. Tater hiked a leg, did his business, then turned towards Jeff's daughter for his reward. His daughter told him he hadn't done enough, and Tater responded by again hiking his leg to earn his reward.

MARKING INSIDE THE HOUSE

Male Marking

People who own male dogs quickly figure out that intact males are more likely to mark inside a house than neutered males. Intact or not, there are several motivators behind male marking. Marking is a communication tool. The urine scent announces a dog's presence in an area. Males will mark as a statement of ownership. Some will mark when they get excited about seeing another dog pass by a window. Dogs will also mark because they feel insecure. A dog who is feeling frustrated will mark, as will a dog who is feeling stressed. Separation anxiety is one factor that stresses out a dog and can cause marking in the house.

An up-and-coming issue is when an intact male encounters an intact female, especially if the female is in heat. Although the male may never have marked in the house before, when the male encounters a female in heat, that leg gets lifted. Now that people are considering keeping their dogs intact for health benefits, this issue looms in their future. No matter what initiates a dog to mark inside the house, once the habit is established, you need to take the right approach to solve this issue.

Although this may begin to sound like a mantra when it comes to house training, it rings true here as well: Don't try to use punishment to reform a dog who marks. Granted, this may occasionally work for a few dogs, but more often, punishment can create a dog who becomes insecure with the owner, or a dog who learns to become sneaky about the habit.

To reform a male dog who marks, you will need to be diligent. Begin by buying a black light, which can be found online or at your local pet supplier. This handheld device allows you to identify all the areas where the dog has marked inside the house. Be aware that a room needs to be fairly dark when you go on your search. Once you locate areas aglow from previously deposited dog urine, you need to completely eliminate the odor with an enzymatic cleaner. If you have a lot of soiled areas on your carpet, you may want to hire a carpet-cleaning service that specializes in removing pet odors.

If you find that your dog tends to mark excessively in certain areas, you can use a product such as Boundary Guard to repel the dog from a particular place. This product needs to be applied at least once a day. You may need to establish a repelling area a foot or two away from the targeted zone in the initial stages of retraining. As the dog begins to stay away from the marking area, you can use the repellent more specifically on the target spot. If the chemical boundary guard doesn't work, try to find a way to secure a physical boundary around the area the dog marks.

Once you've cleaned up all soiled areas and have established barriers around frequented spots, you need to put a girdle on the dog. Some people use a belly band, which goes around the dog's waist and catches urine when a male attempts to mark. I've made my own belly band using a strip of blue jean material and a couple of safety pins to attach some Velcro. A feminine napkin is used to contain any attempts the dog makes to mark. Preventing a dog from marking helps in several ways. The dog's failure to mark begins to discourage this behavior, and he has the urine next to him instead of on target. Some males do not like this feeling.

I've used this technique on several dogs to eliminate male marking, including Albert. At first, I used the band inside his crate to teach him not to mark the corners of the crate. Of course, I first thoroughly cleaned up the crate and his bedding with enzymatic cleaner. The belly band got him to quit that habit. When Albert was allowed to roam my home, I always kept a belly band on him. He had quickly learned what the word "no" meant, and if I saw him hike a leg when he had that belly band on, I'd gently tell him no, then coax him outside. I'd put him out for a short while, knowing full well he probably wouldn't go outside during that time. After all, he wasn't needing to relieve himself, he was simply leaving his calling card.

It took several months before Albert learned not to hike his leg in the house. Once I noticed the belly band was turning up dry most of the time, I kept it on for a few more weeks. He did occasionally have a bit of pee from time to time. After a month of him having a dry belly band, I removed the device. However,

I kept a close watch on him. One day, he seemed to "forget" himself, and he hiked a leg on a recliner. I told him "no, no" in almost a singsong tone. If I'd have shown anger, this sensitive dog would have been upset. By correcting with a nonpunitive tone, I got him to stop and think about what I was trying to communicate. By letting him "think" this through, I gave this dog who liked to please people time to get it. I didn't have any more problems with him after that. He also didn't mark when he went to his forever home.

When it comes to male marking, each dog will have his own journey. With some, you need to eliminate the incentive. If the dog is intact, you will most likely need to use a belly band when a female is in heat. If the dog marks when other dogs come over, make sure you prevent both dogs from marking inside the house. You may want to put them both outside at first, then place a belly band on them while they are inside. If you see them hike a leg, even if they have on a belly band, verbally disagree with that action. Just be sure not to be harsh. If the dog does this a second time, put him outside for a time-out. Replace the soiled urine catch-pad before putting the belly band back on.

While working to train your dog the correct place to go, you may want to put him outside as soon as another dog comes to visit. Have your dog on a leash in anticipation of the other dog's arrival, so you are ready to take the dog right outside. This can help train the dog that outside is where marking belongs. I've seen some dogs actually ask to go outside to mark when another dog comes over.

If your dog tends to sneak away to mark when other dogs come over, you may have an insecurity marker. A dog who marks from insecurity has a different goal than the egotistical-marking dog. The insecurity marker hikes a leg with the attitude, "I'm here, okay? Back off—please." The dog more often tends to sneak away to do this marking. Some may also eliminate in the house. With this dog, in the long run, you will need to work to build confidence in the dog and may need to do more socializing of the dog outside of the house.

To change a marking habit in an insecure dog, you need to assess the dog's level of discomfort about other dogs visiting. If the dog feels secure in a crate, put him in a crate when another dog comes over. If you don't want to use a crate, put the dog on a leash and keep him with you. Don't pick the dog up, but instead use some of the soothing touch techniques talked about in chapter eight as well as some of the other confidence-building techniques in this book. By building confidence in the dog, you can remove the dog's need to mark. Don't hesitate to use a belly band if you feel you need to during the training process.

Female Marking

Females can mark inside a house just like males. I've seen females get into marking contests. Some will even mark food dishes. Intact females are more prone to marking than spayed females. If you find you are having problems with your female marking, you can use similar solutions as discussed with male dogs. There are "britches," or "dog diapers," that are designed for females in heat. These can be employed much like a belly band to help in retraining your female dog.

CHAPTER 4

Emotional House-Training Issues and Overly Submissive Behaviors

From dogs not able to "hold" things very long due to stress to the issue of separation anxiety, not all eliminations in the house are simple house-training issues. Many house-training issues can be more accurately labeled as emotionally driven issues. Sometimes the emotion driving the house training is fear. Other times, the issue develops from the wrong kind of relationship. A few emotionally driven house-training problems were touched upon in the previous chapter. For example, the fearful dog who marks when other dogs come inside the home can be an emotional issue, if the marking was done out of insecurity. To help resolve the dog's problems, the dog needs to learn to feel more secure about other dogs. When you are dealing with emotionally fueled house-training issues, you may need to do more than retrain the dog. The relationship between dog and owner may need to be changed.

HOUSE-TRAINING REGRESSION

Sometimes a dog becomes almost reliably house-trained, only to regress. Dogs, put outside after being in their crate, have come back inside the house to do their business. Other times, a dog who was reliable begins to develop issues. You come home to an unwelcome surprise on the carpet even if you were only gone a few hours. Perhaps a dog you just adopted was reported as reliably house-trained, but unfortunately, you see no supporting evidence of the dog knowing what to do. No matter what causes house-training regression, the issue is very frustrating. The problem can range from occasional to chronic. By handling the situation the correct way, you can resolve the issue.

If your dog is house-trained or almost house-trained when things fall apart, you may be dealing with an emotional issue. I've provided a few cases of house-training regression that can help you sort through your issues and find a solution if your dog has regressed.

If in Doubt, Check It Out

Sometimes behavior is not driving a house-training problem. Certain medical issues can result in unwanted eliminations in the house. If you have a dog who was reliably house-trained but begins to have accidents, your first course of action should be to have the problem checked out by a veterinarian. Bladder infections are one of many reasons why a dog may no longer be able to hold his or her urine. There are a host of other ailments that can cause incontinence issues.

Chip's House-Training Regression

Chip, part Jack Russell terrier and part Chihuahua, was about as cute as a dog could come. When Sam and his wife, Rose, purchased this little dog as a puppy, they found his personality was very lovable and very playful. Unfortunately, Chip developed a problem. At about six months of age, he was becoming almost reliable in his house training but then regressed. His owners tried everything. They'd crate him while they were gone during the day. When they came home, they'd let him out in the backyard, where he'd run around and pee. Unfortunately, when they let him inside, he'd poop. They began to leave him out longer and longer. Sometimes that worked, but often it didn't. For whatever reason, Chip seemed determined to relieve himself in the house.

I was scheduled to consult on this issue; however, a family emergency occurred before I arrived. Rose, who was expecting a baby in a month, was rushed to the hospital with problems. Sam, overseas on a business trip, scrambled to get a flight home. Since my husband was a coworker of Sam's, I was asked to let Chip out that evening. Of course, I was glad to help, but I also went prepared to work with Chip on his problem about eliminating in the house.

I loaded a baggy with several small pieces of cooked steak, then grabbed my warmest jacket and drove twenty-five miles to their house. Using their hidden key to get inside, I was glad to find that Chip hadn't had an accident in his crate. I immediately let him outside and followed him into the backyard. Chip looked relieved as he hiked a leg on a tree. Afterwards, this small dog ran to the back door and waited. But, I was not about to let him in. I walked over to the other end of the yard and called him to me, then coaxed him to walk beside me along the fence, far away from that back door.

Chip walked with me for a little while, then ran back to the door and brushed his paw on it, wanting inside. He still hadn't done his business. I again tried to coax him to me for a walk, knowing full well that exercise such as walking helps stimulate a dog to get the job done. Chip went back to the door and insisted to be let inside. Instead, I picked up a toy and tossed it to get him to play. This little guy loved to play and joined in for a while. Unfortunately, he again returned to the door, this time barking to get inside.

By now, we'd been outside more than half an hour. It was a cold February night, and I also wanted to go inside. But first, Chip had to do his business. I pulled a leash from my pocket and we began to walk along the far fence. I told Chip in a calm voice that all he needed to do was relieve himself outside, and that if it took all night, we'd stay here until he did. The talk was more for me than him.

Finally, just short of an hour outside, Chip could hold it no more. He did his business. The moment he was done, I gave him a bright "good dog, good potty" and shoved a piece of steak towards his mouth. He ate it, so I gave him three more little pieces of steak as a jackpot. Then, we went inside the house.

The baby was born a month early. Fortunately, both mom and baby were fine. Sam got home from the hospital in time to take care of Chip the next morning. I instructed Chip's owners on how to continue his training and emphasized that they needed to go out with the dog. I told them to use a high-value treat and praise his success, as well as allow the dog as much time as he needed. After a week, Chip got over his house-training regression.

Can Human Health Issues Trigger House-Training Regression?

House-training regression typically happens when a dog becomes emotionally upset. Things that can create emotional instability in a dog include changing your or the dog's residence, changes inside the household such as a member leaving the home, and strife inside a household. In Chip's case, I believe he somehow sensed something was wrong with Rose's pregnancy. This theory is based in part on the fact that Chip is very sensitive to people acting angry towards him as well as other human emotions.

Some dogs have been observed to have sensitivities about people that other dogs do not. That is true with seizure-detection dogs. Although a service dog can be trained to detect low blood sugar in people, no one understands why dogs react to an approaching seizure. It is not uncommon for a seizure dog to detect an oncoming seizure hours in advance.

Another example of dogs reacting to people's health is seen with hospice dogs. Years ago I attended a talk by a hospice therapy-dog handler. The woman explained that some dogs would willingly go into a room and could stay with a person about to die, while other dogs did not want to go. Of course, the dog handler never asked the dog to go when the dog didn't want to, because doing so would stress out the dog.

Years later I had another experience with two dogs who reacted very differently to a medical situation. I was called in to see if a dog who'd attacked a family member could be retrained. During my evaluation, I discovered that the six-year-old boy had ADHD. The dog had attacked during one of the boy's episodes. I worked with the family to teach the dog not to attack this boy when he had an episode. However, the boy never got over his fear of this dog so the dog was re-homed.

At the time, one of my fosters was a Chesapeake Bay retriever mix named Shilo. This high-drive, pushy dog had been one of the more challenging dogs I'd ever reformed, but now she was ready to be re-homed. Since Shilo had an exceptionally calm demeanor around people, I thought she might make a good replacement dog for the family.

We arranged a casual meeting with the young boy and Shilo. The boy enjoyed throwing a ball for the dog. At a final meeting before deciding if they should take Shilo home, the boy came over to my house. He said "hi" to the dog, and at his greeting, Shilo began to approach him. Suddenly, the boy became frantic. He cried out in fear and turned around to escape, but was stopped by a wall.

Without a word from me, Shilo stopped and stood calmly. She seemed to understand not to approach the boy. After some soothing words from his mother, the boy settled down. She reminded her son that Shilo was a different dog. When the young boy again spoke to Shilo, she quietly walked towards him. With a little encouragement, he reached out and petted the dog. I knew that Shilo had found the right home.

Sometime later, when I talked to the family to make sure things were still going well with Shilo, the mother told me about something Shilo did. The little boy's grandmother had developed some significant health issues and had to move in with the family. On days the grandmother was feeling especially poorly, Shilo would lie by the bed as if trying to guard the woman from the bad things in the world.

The point of my stories are that dogs react in different ways in regard to people's medical and emotional states. Although I suspect all dogs pick up on our moods and our issues, some dogs tolerate our problems while others may need training to learn to cope. Sometimes a dog will develop issues such as house-training regression, such as Chip did. Often to solve house-training regression, removing the trigger for the regression as well as retraining helps solve the issue. No matter why a dog has a regression issue, never become frustrated or punitive with the dog. Instead, find a way to help the dog learn how to move on from the issue.

Rescue Dogs Who Get Stuck in House-Training Regression

In the previous chapter, you learned how to help rescue dogs acclimate to your home and get over minor house-training problems. However, some rescue dogs can have more chronic house-training issues. There are a variety of reasons rescues can regress with house training. Some were never reliably trained, and that may be part of the reason the dog ended up in rescue. Dogs in a rescue situation can become very insecure, and that insecurity sets up a dog for separation anxiety issues such as Ebony, a dog you will meet in a story below, suffered. Rescue dogs, new to a household, may be fearful or feel very stressed in this new environment. Stress, from fear or other reasons, makes a dog need to go more often.

If you suspect the problem is that the dog was never reliably house-trained to begin with, you can treat the dog like one who was never house-trained. Use some of the guidelines in the previous chapter, including employing the use of a crate. Reward the dog for the correct behavior outside, and don't reprimand any mistakes. Be patient and persistent.

Dogs who have not learned how to hold things all day long because they had access to a doggy door can also benefit from the use of a crate during the retraining process. To help achieve success more quickly, put such a dog on a strict feeding schedule. Feed the dog at the same time each day. First thing in the morning, take the dog outside, allowing enough time to walk the dog until he eliminates. Put the dog in the crate for the day, since the lower activity level can help the dog hold things longer. When you come home, take the dog from the crate directly outside and walk until he relieves himself. During this training time, feel free to offer a treat for each success. At bedtime again put the dog out one last time. If the dog has accidents during the night, use a crate at that time. Once the dog begins to eliminate quickly when you take him outside, you can simply put the dog out and make sure he does his business before coming back inside. Typically you only need to keep up this routine for about a week, especially if you keep the process positive so the dog doesn't feel stressed.

In general, it is best to keep a dog on a regular feeding schedule. Free choice is never recommended unless prescribed by a veterinarian for unique situations. Free-feeding works against house-training efforts and can result in an overweight dog, and some dogs may suddenly engorge, resulting in an emergency condition known as bloat.

If part of your problem is that your new dog is too easily feeling stressed and insecure, you will need to work on building

71

a secure and confident relationship with this dog. Dogs who are feeling insecure will often have their tail tucked and may retreat under tables or corners where they feel more out of sight. One way to help build security in a dog is to do leadership training with the dog, which is covered in chapter nine. Until the dog gets over insecurity issues that are driving house-training regression or if the dog needs training to learn to hold things, use a crate when you are not able to monitor the dog. Be prepared to accompany the dog outside until he becomes comfortable doing his business outside.

SEPARATION ANXIETY

Some house-training issues are a result of mild separation anxiety. The telltale sign is that the dog seems to eliminate primarily when left alone in the house. Dogs who have separation anxiety issues may mark or leave messes on the carpet even if you put them out just before your departure.

Sometimes a dog will develop separation anxiety after you take a vacation. Instead of taking up destructive behaviors more commonly associated with separation anxiety, the dog begins to have house-training issues. This was the case with a Labrador mix named Ebony. Ebony was the only dog in the household. Hanna had owned the dog for five years when this regression happened. Shortly after Hanna came back from a vacation, Ebony began occasionally leaving a pile in the living room. The first thing Hanna did was take Ebony to the vet to make sure there was no medical issue. After the dog received the medical "all clear," behavioral issues were investigated.

After obtaining some history and reviewing certain interactions Hanna had with her dog, the vet diagnosed the dog with mild separation anxiety. It isn't unusual for dogs with mild separation anxiety to sometimes chew up items when left alone or to eliminate in the house. Stress is driving both behavioral issues. The dog, feeling insecure, can begin to feel stressed. That stress can create the need for the dog to eliminate, making the dog unable to hold things until the owner gets home. With dogs who chew items as a result of anxiety, the stress the dog feels when isolated urges the dog to find an item he associates with the owner. Still feeling stressed, the dog often chews to relieve that stress.

Hanna actually unknowingly contributed to her dog's issue of separation anxiety with the wrong kinds of interactions. Hanna had a habit of lavishing her dog with high-energy attention before leaving and when coming home. Typical ways people do this is to use a higher pitched voice and gush all over the dog as they tell the dog how much they will miss him while gone. With some dogs, this kind of interaction can ramp up excitement resulting in increased stress. That increase in stress makes the dog all the more insecure about being alone. When the owner walks out the door after overly exciting a dog, some dogs begin to fret about that departure. Adding to the issue is when the owner comes home and gives the dog an overly excited greeting. That kind of greeting can create anticipation while the owner is away. Anticipation can fester into stress, feeding separation anxiety.

The first part of solving Ebony's separation anxiety was to change Hanna's departure and arrival protocol from one that generated stress to a calmer one. Hanna was told to be calm about her departure and minimize her interactions with the dog. With some dogs, simply changing to a calm departure and arrival solves the problems. With other dogs who have developed a habit of fretting when the owner is gone, specialized training can help. One technique called the "I'll be Back" technique teaches the dog to relax about the owner's departure. Information about this technique can be found at www.peggyswager.com.

GREETING OR EXCITEMENT PEEING

Whether you call the problem greeting peeing or excitement peeing, the results are the same. When you go to meet or greet your dog, you end up with splashes of urine as the dog's back end seems engaged in a dance. Often this problem begins as a result of weaker bladder control. Many young dogs can outgrow this problem. However, if handled the wrong way, the problem can take on a life of its own. To solve the problem, the dog-human relationship needs to be correctly structured.

Most dogs begin having this problem around adolescence, which can start around four months of age. Some dogs seem to struggle with bladder control at this age, while others never have this problem. Adding fuel to the urinary fire is that some dogs can become more easily excited during this adolescent period, and that excitement works against bladder control. Dogs who have a genetic predisposition to poor bladder control may struggle with this problem all their lives.

Owners often unintentionally cue this unwanted problem by the way they greet the dog. They come home happy to see their companion. Often, the dog is spoken to in excited, emotional, and high-pitched tones. Dogs who are already excited to see their owners respond to the owner's excitement by becoming all the more excited. The dog's bladder releases urine during that excitement.

To change your dog's greeting or excitement peeing, you first need to change your behavior. Then, you need to retrain the dog. When you first come in contact with your dog, don't greet him at all. Don't speak any words to the dog and don't look at the dog. Instead, adopt an indifferent attitude, kind of a business-as-usual approach. Once you settle down from coming home, go to a couch and sit down. Calmly call the dog over and offer the dog quiet and comforting affection.

The first few times you take this approach, don't be surprised if the dog still splashes out some urine just seeing you. After all, the dog has a habit of greeting you in an excited manner. Don't show disapproval. In fact, don't acknowledge the dog or this action at all. If you find you are having a hard time controlling your anger when your dog loses pee, consider using a belly band or britches on the dog when you are gone. That can help contain the pee when you come home and may help you not get as angry. Getting angry can create more of a problem.

If after a week the dog hasn't improved, try another technique. When you first come in, calmly stick a treat the dog really likes under the dog's nose and lure him straight outside. Give the dog an opportunity to get rid of any extra urine. When you are ready to calmly greet the dog, let the dog back inside. Greet the dog as described above while sitting quietly on the couch.

If your dog has issues with greeting pee around guests, crate the dog until the household settles down. Be prepared to coach your guest on the correct, low-key mannerisms to use when interacting with your dog. Preferably, have the guest greet the dog while he or she is sitting down, rather than bending over the dog.

Habits take time to change, so be patient with this. Also, if your dog is under a year old and has this habit, the dog may not have enough bladder control for complete success until he gets older. Some things you can do to help out your dog include never using a higher-pitched voice when interacting with the dog, and don't show disapproval to the dog in regard to this issue.

Bailey's Greeting Peeing Issues

Bailey was just over a year old when he came over to my house for a weeklong board-and-train. This male golden retriever had insufficient socialization when young and had not been taken to any training classes. His lack of socialization created behavior problems, and he had to be isolated at doggy day-care. His owners' main complaint was the dog's fear-based leash reactivity. However, his owners mentioned that when-ever they came to pick him up from doggy daycare, the dog would get so excited the moment he saw them, he'd pee all over.

After working with Bailey for a week on his fear issues and leash reactivity, I came up with a plan for when his owners came to take him home. I asked them to park outside of my home and call me when they arrived. I took Bailey outside, but didn't go directly up to the car. Instead, I let him glance in their direction, then led him in a circle. I'd take a few steps towards the car, but if Bailey showed any increased excitement, I'd make another circle. I made a lot of circles to get to their vehicle. This allowed Bailey the opportunity to diffuse his excess excite-ment, and he greeted his owners calmly. Not a single drop had leaked out.

SUBMISSIVE PEEING

Some people think that submissive peeing is the same as excite-ment peeing or what is also called greeting peeing. This is under-standable in that the dog often pees when people go to greet him. But what drives submissive peeing is quite different. Sub-missive peeing can also begin during canine adolescence and is often cued by people when they greet a dog. However, the dog is not at all feeling excited when the human approaches. The dog is reacting in an insecure and overly submissive manner.

A typical scenario is that the person walks up to the dog, then bends over the dog while reaching downwards with the intention of petting him. Some dogs view this looming approach to petting more like a "posturing" behavior, and they respond by showing submission. In dog culture, peeing is a reverent way to show submission.

What Is Posturing?

A dog who postures over another dog does so to intimidate that other dog. When posturing, the dog set on intimidating the other dog will often stand tall, tense his muscles, and may place his head over the back or neck of the dog being asked to take a subordinate position. If a dog feels that a person is looming over him when that person goes to pet him, the dog may feel as if the person is asking him to submit or act submissively. Peeing is one of the strongest ways a dog can show submission.

Breaking an Unwanted Submissive Cycle

Sadly, submissive peeing goes from miscommunication to an unwanted cycle of behavior where floors suffer liquid assaults. Often, people who don't understand that they've just received a "gift" of submission from a dog react the wrong way. Anger at the dog having just peed is common. Your anger towards the dog is quickly interpreted as disapproval. But the dog doesn't see your disapproval in the way you intended. The dog doesn't think you are mad about the peeing, the dog thinks you are mad that the peeing wasn't done well enough, meaning the dog didn't subordinate adequately. What often happens next is that the dog will pee more quickly or a little longer the next time you approach. If you again react with disapproval, you set up a cycle where the dog not only becomes stressed, but feels you are telling him to try harder to appease you with his pee.

Breaking a dog of submissively peeing takes several steps. First, you need to refuse the behavior. To do that, you break any eye contact and stop any attempt to touch the dog. Keep your attitude amiable. This tells the dog you do not want this gift of groveling. The second thing you do is train the dog how to interact with you without peeing. Keep in mind the dog often cues to submissively pee when a person bends over to pet him. Avoid looming or bending to greet a dog. Instead, lower to the dog's level. A lot of dogs will welcome contact on their chest when you first greet them.

If the dog rolls onto his back or crouches at your approach, take that as your cue to stop your approach. Calmly turn around, walk a step or so away, and sit, preferably on the floor. Call the dog over to you. When the dog arrives, offer affection by first rubbing the dog's chest. Once the dog relaxes, you can rub behind the ears, working your way to the top of the head. When talking to the dog, use a comforting tone. Higher-pitched tones tend to unnerve dogs who are feeling uncertain.

By petting the dog at a lower level rather than looming, you can teach the dog to accept the attention without offering you a gift of submission. Once the dog gets comfortable with your attention, you can begin to teach the dog to come to you for attention. Once the dog better understands the relationship you want, you can begin to desensitize the dog to your bending to pet him.

When working to train a dog to let you bend and greet, the first time or two that you call the dog over, watch how he approaches you. Some dogs will want to approach you submissively by crawling or lowering their head or tail. This is not the right moment to greet the dog. If the dog tries this kind of approach, break that cycle by tossing a small treat in front of the dog. Once the dog learns to approach less reluctantly, you can continue your training. Again you will use a treat. A good kind is one that you can hold while the dog works to eat the treat; for instance, a large biscuit. Hold out the treat and call the dog forward. Once the dog is crunching on the biscuit, reach towards him. If the dog crouches or acts unsure in any way, stop where you are and toss a small piece of food. Repeat the process by asking the dog to come at least one step forward to again eat the biscuit. Even if it takes several tries to be able to bend towards the dog, be patient. Once the dog begins to accept your bending towards him for a greeting, pet the dog on the chest. Work your way up to petting the top of the head. As far as petting the dog on top of the head, some dogs never feel comfortable with that, while others adjust more quickly. Either way, you don't want to try petting the head until the dog becomes very calm about you reaching downwards.

When handled correctly, most dogs will outgrow submissive peeing by a year of age. Older dogs who have an overly submissive nature can also learn to be less submissive and more confident with the right training and by working to build the dog's self-assurance. Playing with the dog and becoming a partner with the dog are a couple of ways to help build the dog's self-confidence. You can learn how to build more confidence in your dog by doing the leadership training described in chapter nine.

Don't Approach an Overly Submissive Dog

When you are first working to break an overly submissive cycle, don't approach the dog. Instead, call the dog to you. Overly submissive dogs who are insecure will too quickly retreat into a submissive action. Conversely, you will find that getting the dog to move forward helps to break the overly submissive cycle. Although it sounds simple, following these rules can quickly build the right kind of relationship between dog and owner. Since an overly submissive relationship creates an insecure dog and insecure dogs become more fearful, breaking a submissive pattern will help build security in your dog.

Kayla Had Issues at Eight Weeks

Jane felt that Kayla was a great dog, smart and intelligent, but this little terrier's peeing was frustrating for her and her husband, Dave. "You go to take off her leash and she pees," Jane reported. "We love her and are happy with her, except for the peeing." Jane explained that Dave got so frustrated when the dog peed that he'd rub Kayla's nose in it. Instead of learning to stop peeing, things only got worse, until anytime Dave tried to pet the dog, she'd pee. These dog owners told me that if this didn't stop, they weren't going to keep Kayla.

I told Jane and Dave that there was hope, but they'd have to be patient. How patient they needed to be I couldn't predict, because Kayla's success was dependent on Dave's learning to find patience with the dog and to stop acting in a negative and disapproving manner.

We talked over what they needed to do to change Kayla's behavior. I told them they had to eliminate any kind of reprimands. Instead of punishing or scolding for unwanted behaviors, they needed to train for behaviors they wanted. As well, we talked about the right tone of voice. They mentioned once having picked the dog up by the scruff and she'd peed quite a lot. I pointed out that this action only added fuel to the submissive dog's fire.

We also talked about unsnapping Kayla's leash. What they needed to do was to go down to the dog's level and scratch the dog's chest. Once the dog relaxed, they could reach behind her neck and remove the leash. I then suggested they play with the dog. Dogs often abandon their submissive behaviors when they play and learn to enjoy a more positive interaction with their owners.

I didn't hear from Jane for a few months. When she called, Jane said that Kayla got better right away about the leash issue. They were working on Dave and Kayla's relationship when a new issue came up. At first when Dave played with Kayla, it went well and the dog seemed to warm up to Dave. Then, Kayla began to pee when she played, and Dave was again losing his patience.

80

I told them they might be dealing with both excitement peeing and submissive peeing issues. I reminded them that neither issue should receive attention, especially not negative attention. I suggested something to try. When Kayla started to pee while playing, they were to stop the play session. Once Kayla settled down, they could try again. If Kayla again peed, they needed to end the session without any kind of disapproval and not try to play until the next day. I also told them that since Kayla was under a year old, she might need more time to develop good control of peeing when excited.

That was the last I heard from Jane for a very long time, and I often wondered if they kept this dog. Then one day, Jane e-mailed me: "Well after a year of not petting her (unless outside) she stopped the peeing. Kayla just jumped on my hubby's lap one day in the house, and viola, peeing gone (well almost completely, gets excited and loses control once in a while, but not like it was happening). Thought you might like to know. Thanks for your assistance again and we did not give up on her."

Help for Kayla

Years later, I was talking over the case and resolution of Kayla's submissive issues with a trainer. She suggested using a belly band, or britches for females, as discussed in chapter three. The idea was twofold. First, the pee smell itself with a belly band or britches is muted and may not give the dog the feedback he or she seeks, thus discouraging this attempt to submit. Also important is that if Kayla had donned britches, Dave may have not lost his patience as quickly since his carpet didn't get soiled. Kayla's success was dependent upon retraining Dave's behavior.

UNWANTED CUES THAT CAN CAUSE OVERLY SUBMISSIVE BEHAVIORS

Although you may not mean to do so, you can actually cue a dog to display overly submissive behavior. Below is a list of the common ways people unintentionally cue a dog, along with ways to help resolve the issue. These cues can also add to a dog's fearfulness and insecurity, even if the dog doesn't submissively pee.

Eye Contact

The wrong eye contact can trigger an overly submissive reaction in a dog. The worst kind of eye contact is a stern stare. Couple that with stern facial features and you are asking your dog to feel insecure about you. Some dogs seem to have very little tolerance for your looking directly at them, especially if the dog is soft. With these dogs, you will often find the dog reacts in a more relaxed manner if you look at the ground as you approach. If you do happen to make eye contact with an uncertain dog, glance sideways. That tells the dog you don't have hostile intentions. Once the dog begins to break the overly submissive behaviors, you may be able to make mild eye contact. Mild eye contact is where you have a soft gaze and a peaceful look on your face.

Speed and Direction of Your Approach

With some dogs, walking directly towards them can be deemed as a threat. Rushing up to an insecure dog will invite the dog to flee. If you are dealing with an insecure or submissive dog, don't directly approach the dog. Instead, meander up as if preoccupied with something else. Dogs who are trying to communicate an amiable approach will travel in an arc one way and then the other way when nearing a strange dog. The dog will also sniff the ground. Although you can't sniff the ground, you can act as if you are paying attention to the ground and not the dog.

This is an acceptable way to approach a dog who is uncertain about you.

Body Posture

Both looming and standing rigidly over a dog can intimidate the dog. Dogs will also notice if you have a stiff posture. If the muscles in your shoulders are tense and your head is too rigid, the dog can become uncertain.

Voice

Some dogs are very reactive to harsh tones of voice. A stern "no" can make a sensitive dog quake. Likewise, a higher-pitched tone, if the dog is feeling uncertain, can work against security in a dog. A lot of times people mistakenly use a motivational tone of voice when looking to reassure a dog. This kind of tone more often unnerves a dog. It is best to use an even, self-assured tone. Think about what kinds of tones make you feel more secure. Dogs typically respond the same way.

FEAR PEEING

Some dogs can become so afraid of you that they actually pee out of fear. Even dogs who begin with submissive peeing can change to fear peeing or do a combination of both if you punish them. A lot of the time, people confuse overly submissive behaviors as indications that dogs were abused. Overly submissive behaviors tend to be more about the dog's basic nature than the dog's ever being abused.

I have seen some dogs pee out of fear. One such dog was Jewel, a German shepherd mill dog rescue I fostered. This dog never had any accidents inside the house, nor did she pee if you reached down towards her. Her house-training reliability was admirable. One day she was lying in the living room of my house, and in the adjoining kitchen, I used a flyswatter to hit a fly. Jewel ran down the hallway and stopped outside a closed bedroom door. There she peed. Like most dogs, Jewel was an enormously forgiving dog and with the right treatment was willing to forgive people's past transgressions. However, someone had at one time struck her, and I'm willing to bet more than once. She had peed at the end of that hall because she felt she was cornered and feared she was going to be hit. This was not a house-training issue, but a fear issue. With a lot of dogs who have this kind of issue, typical desensitizing techniques are used. With this highly fearful mill dog rescue, she first needed work on learning to trust me. Part of that work involved using the soothing touch, which is discussed in chapter eight.

CHAPTER 5

Bringing Home a Fearful Dog

For people who have just acquired a fearful dog, the sooner they work to resolve the dog's fears, the better. The easiest kind of dog to help feel secure is one who had a secure upbringing but became insecure due to a rescue environment. Unfortunately, some fearful dogs have never had the opportunity to feel secure. From under-socialization to more-challenging natures that were not worked with correctly, dogs who have not learned a sense of security pose an extra challenge and may need extra help to acclimate to your home. The two mill dogs I took on for reform were more extreme cases. However, looking at what worked in their reform can help people who get stuck with fearful dogs they've just brought home.

PUPPY MILL BREEDING DOGS

Puppy mill breeding dogs live their lives inside a small wire crate with several other dogs. Larger dogs are either housed in a hutch or an outside pen. The people come by from time to time and grab the dog out of the cage in a manner which by itself can be frightening, take the dog somewhere, and after doing something unpleasant to the dog, shove the dog back into his cage.

This is only one of many frightening experiences puppy mill breeding dogs may encounter. Dog rescue organizations see all sorts of horrors from puppy mill facilities. In the state where I live, one breeding facility owner was nicknamed the "Power-Wash Lady." This woman's facility used a power-wash to clean up the kennels. Some of the smaller dogs who were "cleaned" in this way lost eyes. Other dogs must have felt as if they were being waterboarded.

Typically, mill dogs live in a highly fearful state during most of the daylight hours, fretting every time someone comes close to the cage. At night, when things quiet down and the people are not around to hurt them, these dogs finally have an opportunity to feel somewhat safe. And although the cage is not a great place, the dog quickly learns that the world outside of the cage is much worse.

RESCUE DOGS

Insecure dogs that come from a rescue often find the rescue environment very stressful. The noises and missing comforts of home can leave the dog shaken. Even dogs who are secure and comfortable in the world outside of a rescue can become unnerved by the rescue environment. Secure dogs may feed off of the insecure dogs' fears. Some dogs in a no-kill facility may spend months and months in a cage awaiting adoption.

Though issues that result in dogs becoming excessively stressed or fearful are unintentional, the consequences of a dog in a rescue can result in the dog having challenges adapting to your home. To overcome your dog's security challenges, you may need to work to gradually introduce the dog into your household.

BEGINNING YOUR DOG'S JOURNEY

When people encounter dogs who have suffered at the hands of other humans or are missing out on a happy life, it is human nature to want to make up for any misfortune the dog has encountered. Likewise, if you have a highly fearful dog, you may be tempted to become overly protective. However, for your dog to begin his journey to a happier life, the dog must learn how to feel secure. So if you set your dog free inside your home only to find the dog is not comfortable sleeping at your feet and interacting with the family, you will need to take steps to resolve that issue. While it's true the sooner you begin that process the better, even if your dog has hidden under beds or behind couches for years, you can help the dog become more secure in your home. Although each dog will have a little different journey to learning to relax in a household, below I've provided information on what worked for Otis and Albert and for Emma.

OTIS AND ALBERT'S HOUSING ARRANGEMENTS

When I first brought Otis and Albert home, I didn't turn them loose in my house and hope for the best. Instead, I put them in a very large wire cage as their first home. This may surprise some people. After all, that kind of housing was for too long the bane of their existence. However, I knew they needed something they were familiar with to learn to become less afraid in a home. This was the first time they'd lived inside a house. They needed to learn that the different noises, smells, and people in this place were all safe to them. By beginning their journey in a crate, somewhere they knew they could survive, they could more easily learn to get used to a home.

I wanted to keep them in a cage that was larger than any I owned, so I borrowed one from a friend. I needed the extra-large cage so I could set up a doggy RV, which is described in chapter three. The cage had a wire bottom and a tray underneath and was about two by four feet in size. If I were to buy a cage to do this kind of thing, I would purchase a cage with a solid bottom. Even though I had covered almost all of the wire with a more comfortable surface for them to walk on, I had issues with the wire bottom. I found the flimsy wire didn't allow me to crawl in though the front to pick up the dogs when I needed to. Instead, I had to lean over the top to try to get the dog out of the farthest corner to pick him up. Not being as tall as some people, I had a hard time picking up the dogs this way. The challenges of picking up a dog at so close to the limit of my reach may have had me come across as less steady than I'd have liked. Anything that looks like uncertainty when interacting with a dog will make the dog feel less secure about what you are doing.

If you have a larger dog, you may want to secure a quiet corner in a room and place a bed or something else for the dog to lie on. Another option is to purchase an exercise pen to confine the dog or a large kennel. Providing a refuge for a dog in the early stages of welcoming him into your home is very beneficial to a less-secure dog, because this gives the dog an opportunity to begin to feel more secure in your house. Some fearful dogs will need time to get used to your being around and the sounds and commotions in your household. Although you will eventually transition the dog into your household, with highly fearful dogs, that process will take time.

Otis and Albert's Day One

When I first got home with these two mill dog rescues, I put the dogs in a quiet room as joint tenants in their self-contained cage. They were left alone for the rest of the day, other than me walking through to look in on them and refresh their food and water. Since Otis and Albert had such an extreme fear of people, not trying to interact with them a lot had an advantage. They could spend more time settling down about the new place without being concerned about me.

If you have a rescue who is uncertain, this arrangement can be helpful. When you do decide to interact with the dog, consider doing very little with the dog at first. Although you may want to shower your dog with affection, it is better to sit quietly nearby and read a book. That allows the dog to take his time getting used to you, without worrying about being touched. Remember, many less-secure dogs are uncertain when people touch them until they get to know the person better. Quietly reading nearby allows the dog to take his time relaxing about your presence. You may want to drop a treat in the cage before walking away to facilitate the dog liking your company.

Albert's Forever Home

Security is a foundation you build in your dog. The more positive experiences you give the dog that allow him to feel secure, the more quickly you free your dog from fear. However, too often we are dealing with dogs who are missing out on a secure foundation.

Three of Albert's first four years of life before he came to my home were in a very bad puppy mill. During the next year at the rescue facility, he remained so afraid that he felt the need to bite to defend himself. At my home, I worked with him for three-quarters of a year. Still, this only allowed him one place in the entire world to feel secure. Then, he was again uprooted to a new home with four people and two dogs he didn't know.

Fortunately, Albert's new owner, Jina, knew how to best acclimate this dog. For the first week, she wrapped him in a blanket and put him on her son's bed. Each night Jina's son read to Albert for about an hour. This did the trick for this Chihuahua. From time to time, Albert is known to still drag that blanket to Jina for her to fold up so he can lie on it.

Otis and Albert's Day Two

The next day, when I came in with their food, both dogs retreated to the bed at the back of the crate. I had brought a few small pieces of turkey. Albert was always the bolder of the two and led the way to stretching forward to snatch that treat. Otis stayed as far away as possible. At first Otis turned his head away. But I am good at breaking turkey into very small pieces,

89

so I could offer Albert several. I patiently held out a piece for Otis all the while, and he finally glanced at me. For the second day, that wasn't so bad for Otis. Of course, since I was home all day, I could do this more than once.

I had a hard time offering Otis treats, making me wish he was the only dog in the cage. To help Otis get over his fear of accepting a treat from me, if he had been the only dog, I'd have simply left the treat nearby and walked away. This would have allowed Otis a chance to decide that I came for good reasons, such as giving him a treat. As it was, Albert didn't hesitate to eat any and all treats I tried to leave for Otis.

If you are working with a very reluctant dog like Otis, and that is the only fearful dog you are working with, try leaving the treat and walking away. But keep a watch over your shoulder. If the dog takes a step forward to eat the treat before you are out of sight, that is great progress. If the dog will not move from his corner until after you are gone, that is fine. The first goal is to get the dog to eat the treat you left.

Eventually you will find that the dog, as long as you turn away after you leave the treat, will begin to venture forward sooner. You can look over your shoulder after you turn away to leave, and once the dog begins to move forward, try stopping and standing with your back to the dog. Once the dog eats a treat while you stand nearby, you can work to lure the dog to the treat while you hold it. Even if you have to drop it in front of the dog to begin with, if the dog will come forward without your having to turn your back, you are making great progress. But don't stare at the dog at any time. Make sure you are looking sideways rather than directly towards the dog. In fact, by slightly turning your head sideways, you will be sending what is called a calming signal to the dog. Calming signals are explained in more detail in chapter seven. Some dogs may need a lot of time with this part of the training, but have patience. The dog's moving forward towards you is a great mental achievement in overcoming their fears, and their fears are all mental.

Some Dogs Recover Faster Than Others

After about a week, I began to pick up Otis and Albert and put them in the front pen. Watching them play in that small pen was entertaining. This was their first time outside, and they acted as if the small pen was the most wonderful place in the world. After they began to go on walks, that pen was seen as a bit boring. Over the next few weeks, they became secure enough with my presence that I could do "come" training with Albert, which is discussed in chapter nine.

I did more work with Albert, since he more quickly got over his fearfulness. Otis was a slow grind when it came to making progress, and you'll learn more about the extra help he needed in the next chapter. Although individual dogs are different, you'll find there are two factors that will make a difference in your efforts to free them from fears. The first is the dog's base personality, and the second is the kind of fearful situations that particular dog was exposed to. By using the right efforts for your particular dog, you will find success. So even if someone else you know had an easier time than you, don't be discouraged. Time and the right technique will win out in the end.

EMMA'S SECOND CHANCE

The first I heard about Emma, a mill dog rescue, was through an e-mail: "Emma, a cocker spaniel, will be returned to the kennel by June 15th. After six months, the owner had no luck with her rehab, and the dog is still very timid. If you can help this sweet chocolate Cocker Spaniel girl learn to trust and love please let me know."

After Otis and Albert had found their forever homes, I felt ready to take on another mill dog rescue. After reading the e-mail about Emma, I very much wanted to work with her to see if what I'd learned from working with Otis and Albert could more quickly help out this dog. Although another foster took her on before I could offer, I worked with both the foster and then her forever home to help Emma come out of her shell.

I did learn some of the reasons why Emma didn't work out in her initial home. Although her adoptive owners meant well, Emma was never allowed any time to acclimate to her new home. Adding to the dog's problems was the owner's seven-year-old child. The child wanted to shower the dog with love. Anytime Emma wasn't completely hidden away, he'd enthusiastically run up to hug the dog. Emma quickly learned to stay in hiding during the day, only sneaking out at night to eat. Hiding all of the time didn't allow her to become house-trained. Since her new owners did not provide her with a sanctuary when she first arrived, Emma came up with her own by finding areas in the house where she could vanish from sight. Unfortunately, she failed to progress away from any of her fears, and if anything, they were reinforced and perhaps expanded.

Emma's Foster Home

Emma was lucky that she had the opportunity to go into a foster home instead of having to go back to the mill dog rescue kennels. Dogs do so much better in a foster home than in the rescue's kennel.

Laurel West has fostered mill dog rescues for many years. A lot of the fosters who take on mill dogs use a technique similar to Laurel's because it works for the majority of the dogs. I feel it is important to see how some of the mill dog fosters handle their dogs since these methods can work for a lot of dogs. However, if you are not finding success with the more typical methods, you'll find a lot of other techniques to use in this book.

Laurel turns out most of her mill dogs when they get to her home. She has a doggy door and two terriers who help the newcomers go outside to the pleasant backyard and wander around the house. Laurel takes steps to train the dog to use the doggy door as well. She puts them through the doggy door while using the command "outside."

What Laurel has observed with a lot of the dogs she has fostered is that allowing the dogs the "run of the house" helps them to acclimate to a regular home. Part of the success with these dogs is a result of the "help" her terriers provide.

The dogs soon discover their freedom and love it. Laurel also helps the dogs learn to settle down by picking them up and setting them next to her on the couch. She has them stay with her until they relax so the dogs can learn that hanging out with people is not a bad thing. Laurel understands that she can't let a dog leave the couch and her company until the dog relaxes at least a little about being with her on the couch. If she were to return the dog to the floor before the dog showed a little bit of relaxation, there would not be any progress made in diffusing the dog's fear. Laurel often finds it takes about a month for new mill dogs to settle into her home enough that they become comfortable with her picking them up.

Emma Needed Extra Help

Some dogs have come into a new home, hidden behind the couch or under a bed, and stayed there for years. It isn't unusual for dogs with excessive fear issues to withdraw into their fear worlds, which they cannot escape without help. Emma wanted to hide away in this fashion. Laurel speculated that Emma's adopted family made a few errors that perpetuated the dog's insecurities. She discovered that the only time Emma was allowed outside was for potty times. Those rare times involved the dog being leashed, keeping the dog from exploring her world. Contributing to Emma's issues with the first home was the expectation by her new owners that she could tolerate a child running up. Emma was not the only dog who can find this unnerving. More fearful and less secure dogs often find someone rushing up to them frightening.

When Emma first arrived at Laurel's home, she would hide away more insistently than Laurel's other mill dogs. To prevent this habit, Laurel placed blockades over all the hiding places, such as under beds or behind couches. This can work for some dogs and is a first thing to try. As well, using a quiet area as described earlier can help.

A Nocturnal Nature

Emma, like many mill dogs, would wait until night to sneak outside through the doggy door. Once outside, she didn't want to come back inside. Laurel has seen this in other mill dogs, who will often become nocturnal because they feel safe coming out at night. I speculate that dogs caged inside a puppy mill are often exposed to a lot of fearful stimuli during the day, but find the nights are peaceful. Laurel has commented that once a mill dog realizes he or she is free all of the time, coupled with the less stressful environment of her home, the dog will typically learn to hang out during the day and will discover the ability to go outside anytime at will. Certainly, Laurel's terriers have helped many of the mill dogs feel safer than any person could and showed by example that people are not all that bad.

Unfortunately, Emma just wasn't settling in and remained far too fearful to come out during the day. To help Emma learn to feel safe in a home, I explained to Laurel what I had done for Otis. Otis needed me to build him a sanctuary and slowly acclimate him to my house. Laurel did this for Emma, and things turned around for the dog. You'll find that information in the next chapter.

CHAPTER 6

Codependent Dogs, Vanishing Dogs, and Bed Hiders

Some dog owners already have a dog living in their home who is too fearful to act like a normal dog. These dogs may retreat to a hiding place once you turn them loose in your home. That was what Emma did in her first adopted home. Once she was relinquished back to the rescue and sent to a foster home, she immediately took up her vanishing act. Even after Otis's gentle introduction to home life as described in the previous chapter, he needed extra help learning how to simply hang out with people. Fearful dogs will find hiding places under your bed, behind couches, or in any darker recess they discover. Blocking those areas helps some dogs, but others may need extra help. Although another dog in the household can help a fearful dog transition into a more secure dog, if both dogs develop a codependent relationship, your first step to building a secure relationship with your dog will need to be removing that unhealthy relationship.

REMOVING UNHEALTHY CODEPENDENT RELATIONSHIPS

If you already have a secure dog with a good relationship with you, bringing in a fearful dog often isn't a problem. The secure dog can help teach your insecure dog that you are not to be feared, and the secure dog can help the insecure dog feel more at ease in your household. (Laurel had two terriers at her foster home who helped a lot of dogs acclimate. Of course, Emma became the exception.) However, sometimes the insecure dog will learn to feel secure about your dog, but not about you. Other problems occur when two insecure dogs develop a relationship that supports each other's insecurity. If you have two insecure dogs who are highly dependent on each other, you need to separate those two dogs to build a secure relationship between you and each dog.

I quickly found out with Otis and Albert that they had an unhealthy dependency relationship with each other that shut me out. This relationship worked to support fearfulness in each one. The first time this became apparent was when we had the two dogs out on a walk. Although walks are generally a great way for a dog to bond to people and to settle down in general, if my husband tried to take Otis ahead of me on the walk, Albert would panic. That resulted in Otis becoming frantic. I realized that to help these two dogs become less fearful and more self-secure, I had to keep them completely separated inside my household, not allowing them to know the other dog was anywhere around. Keeping them together allowed them to feed each other's fears.

I separated these two dogs in stages. At first, I put them in two smaller crates which faced each other. Since they could see each other, they didn't fuss about this change. After slowly moving the two crates farther apart, but still keeping one crate in sight of the other, one night I came in and covered up Albert's crate. The next morning, before I uncovered the crate, I removed Otis's crate to another room. This separation did a couple of things: It helped the dogs to begin to feel more secure when by themselves, and it allowed the dogs to learn to bond to a human instead of only bonding to another dog. Once they began to live in separate rooms, I kept them separated all the time. If one was in the house with me, the other one was either in a crate in another room or outside. Both dogs had already grown comfortable being in my front outside pen together, and didn't act insecure when alone in that pen.

Separating Puppies

If you get two puppies from the same litter at the same time, you will greatly benefit by separating them into two different crates. This will teach them independence from each other as well as allow you to work with the dogs as individuals. That individual attention will create a bond with you rather than having the dogs bond to each other. You can separate two puppies in a similar way as I did with Albert and Otis. It is okay the first few days in your home to keep them together, then put them in separate crates facing each other. Keep moving them farther and farther apart. Be sure to allow them time to adjust to each change.

ACCLIMATING A DOG INSIDE YOUR HOUSE

We think of our house as a sanctuary. If you have a mill dog or a fearful rescue, you may need to teach the dog that your entire house is a sanctuary. Otherwise, the dog may look for a hiding place so he or she feels safe. I have known of some fearful dogs who after several years never really ventured out from under beds or other safe areas. With the right kind of help, you can teach an insecure dog to feel safe in your household sanctuary.

There are several ways to get a dog to feel secure in your house. Laurel talked about simply turning out a new foster dog to wander in her house for the first few days, allowing her other, stable dogs to show the new dog the ropes. The new dogs learned from the terriers how to come and go through a dog door (though Laurel will sometimes help the dog with this). The foster dog also had the opportunity to see that the stable dogs didn't feel the need to skitter away from people, and for some dogs, that helps them to learn to relax. Although this can introduce a fearful dog to the right kinds of behaviors, typically people need to do some one-on-one work with the dog to completely reform him. In addition, some people don't have a dog to help acclimate their fearful dog. In these situations, you will need to find different ways to get your dog to feel more stable, which are covered below.

THE LYING ON THE FLOOR TECHNIQUE

There are several ways you can use the "lying on the floor" technique to help diffuse fear and to actually become friends with a dog. Prior to having success with Albert and Otis, when using this technique, I'd have people greeting shyer dogs sit on the floor or partially lie down (head propped up against the couch), or in some way get down to the dog's level to greet a more fearful dog. This worked well, especially with larger and more powerful men who might otherwise intimidate the dog. We used this method with Shay the first time she met my son Scott, and she quickly learned to feel comfortable with him. I felt it was important for them to meet this way because she had immediately become fearful the first time she met my husband, Ken. When Shay first saw Ken standing a short distance away, she reacted fearfully. That initial fearful reaction took a long time to diffuse. Scott was on the floor with his head propped against the couch for his first meeting, and Shay always greeted him after that in an amiable way.

With Otis and Albert, I would lie on the floor for long periods of time, which helped both of them more quickly feel comfortable with me. With Albert, I'd be on the floor while he was learning to hang out in the house. With Otis, I'd lie down next to his crate for hours at a time and read or type on a laptop. I didn't just decide to lie on the floor for extended periods of time to see if that would help a fearful mill dog. Unfortunately, I had to lie on the floor for hours because of a whiplash injury from an auto accident which resulted in my being in pain. Lying on the floor helped the pain go away. However, since this seemed to really help the dogs get over their fear of me, and later other people, I was glad there was some good that came out of that unpleasant experience.

I'd recommend if your dog is having a hard time getting over his or her fear of you, that you try lying on the floor while you watch television or read a book. You can purchase small mats from a camping store to make lying down more comfortable and use pillows for propping up your head.

Albert's Take on the Floor Technique

Albert warmed up to being handled a lot better than Otis did when I first turned him loose in the house. I blocked off the hallway with a gate, and let him hang out with me in the living room while I spent my time on the floor. Although with some dogs you may need to stuff things around hiding areas such as behind couches so they can't hide, I didn't need to do that with Albert.

Before I tried lying on the floor while Albert wandered around my living room, I tried more traditional desensitization techniques. He'd very quickly become too afraid to eat anything, but I did work to get him used to my reaching towards him and scratching his chest area. When I walked around in the living room, Albert kept his distance from me. However, he quickly became comfortable with me at his level when I lay on the floor. While on the floor, I'd talk to Albert and sometimes coax him over with a treat. Soon, he began to allow me to rub a little on his chest because that was his favorite "first" contact point. Before, I had to have a leash attached to touch him at all, and he often pulled back, resisting my contact. As he got more comfortable with my touch, I'd work on rubbing behind his ear and rubbing other parts. Although I never did an official "soothing touch" technique with Al, from the floor I began to get a lot of those areas covered.

Al began to enjoy my working different areas on his body. Anytime I would lie on the floor, he'd come right over for attention. What was meant to be an opportunity to work on diffusing Al's fear of human contact quickly became a problem. I wasn't able to read or anything else. The word *pest* best described him. I began to teach him the command "all done" followed by my refusal to be conned into rubbing him. He kind of obeyed. He figured "all done" meant I needed about a five-minute break, after which he came back for attention. I'd always end up putting him up in a crate or putting him outside to escape him. My husband also became a victim. One time Ken was lying on the couch sleeping with his hand dangled over the side. He woke up to Al nudging him for rubs. In no time at all, floor time created a Chihuahua who was a lot more comfortable interacting with people. However, it did take more work to get him comfortable with us when we stood over him. But this was a good place to begin to build the right kind of new relationship with this dog.

Another Floor Example

Aspen was a dog who came from a regular home and had a lot of socialization from puppyhood onward. This dog's shyness had genetic roots, and it took a lot of work to move her from very shy to her more reserved nature. She was one of two very challenging dogs I did extensive work with who had issues even though they also had had opportunities for adequate socialization. I learned a lot about working with shyness in dogs from these two very challenging cases.

When I re-homed Aspen, the man who took her into his house called me and said she was acting very timid towards him the first night as well as the next day. However, having positive experiences with people as a puppy meant she didn't take long to adjust to her new home. What helped the most happened after the new owner decided to lie on the floor to take a nap. When he awoke, he found Aspen had laid with him and had her muzzle on his chest. They went for a walk later that evening, and from then on, Aspen acted as if they'd been together all their lives.

THE WIRE CRATE TECHNIQUE

When I started working with Otis to acclimate him to staying with me inside the house when no other dogs were around, things didn't go so well. The first time I turned Otis loose in my house, with no Albert around, he became highly stressed. Although Otis didn't scurry out of sight that first day in my living room, he wandered like a lost dog and panted excessively. Heavy panting when a dog is not hot is a sign of stress. When dogs really becomes stressed, they will begin to cup the end of their tongue. I watched Otis for over half an hour in my house. Instead of relaxing during that time, he became more and more stressed until he had that cupped tongue. Time wasn't solving his problem. Otis couldn't handle life outside of the cage without Albert by his side.

To help Otis acclimate to my living room without being so stressed, I used what I now call the "wire crate technique." I put him in a wire crate in the middle of my living room. While he was in this crate, he was exposed to noises from the television and me walking by. Since Otis had lived in a similar crate with people at times passing by, he felt more secure.

I did not do any one-on-one interactions at first, but used the power of ignoring him. What I mean by the power of ignoring him is that when he was in the mill dog environment and people passed by his cage ignoring him, he learned he was safer. If people looked at him or stopped at his cage, typically fearful things happened. By initially ignoring Otis, I gave him the chance to feel secure about being in that crate in that location. He also had the chance to get used to my behaviors without viewing them as ones that would end as bad or scary actions. He learned that my talking didn't mean bad things would happen, that my stopping nearby the cage was okay, and that my walking by wasn't a threat. Otis accepted that inside this crate in my living room (not quite in the center, but not at all in a corner) was an okay place to be and he didn't need to shut down because he was too afraid.

Taking an indifferent attitude towards a dog that is afraid of you, rather than trying to do too much with the dog in the very beginning, can make the transition into your home easier on the dog. Although we want to give them attention, they need to diffuse some of their fear of us before that is going to work very well. So when you first work with a very fearful dog that is uncertain about you, rather than try to approach the dog too much, simply put his crate in an area where you are going to be a lot of the time. Go about your business as if there wasn't a dog in a crate in your living room. As to where you locate that crate depends on the dog. As long as the dog feels secure inside the crate, you can locate the crate in an open area in your living room. After an hour, spy on the dog and make sure he is not tense, panting, or pacing. If you see any of these activities, this is not a good area. You will need to move the crate to a more secluded area to begin with. If the dog is lying down or looking relaxed, you can leave the crate in that area.

Once you find an area where you can crate the dog and have the dog relaxed, take opportunities to walk by the crate. As you begin to notice the dog isn't reacting to you merely walking by the crate, you can initiate more interactions. You might drop in a nice treat for the dog to eat. Don't ask for the dog to do anything in return, and don't linger. Just leave the treat as you pass by. When you notice the dog looks towards you when you bring the treat, or maybe takes a step towards where you put the treat, linger while the dog eats the treat. You can even teach the dog to come to the front of the crate for the treat. If you see the dog beginning to walk your way when you bring the treat, assign a command like "Otis, come," or you can simply say "come." Once you have success with the dog taking a treat associated with the word "come," work to give the command before the dog takes a step towards getting the treat. Don't do any other interaction when teaching the dog to come for a treat.

Choice of Crates

For the mill dogs, I used a wire crate because the dogs were used to being housed in wire crates. Of course, I prefer a solid bottom on the crate for the comfort of the dog. I also liked that the dogs were somewhat exposed in the wire crate, which I felt gave them a chance to get used to my milling around. However, some dogs may do better with a solid-sided crate, at least at first. This is something to try if the dog is not doing well in a wire crate, even if you put the crate in a more secluded area. Another thing to try is using a blanket to partially cover the wire crate. This allows you to locate the crate in a less secluded area, and once the dog settles down about that location, you can begin to gradually remove the cover on the crate.

The Crate, the Floor, and Otis

After a few days of just walking by the crate with Otis in it, I set the crate next to the area where I would lie on the floor. Otis had me lying next to him for hours while he was in the crate. For several days I didn't interact with him, but just let him get used to me being that close for so long. Finally I'd stick food through the crate. This helped him learn to relax a lot more around me. I continued to drop food in his crate when I walked by. One day I noticed he actually wagged his tail at my approach, albeit a brief wag. During this time when his crate was in the same room that my husband and I walked by, we were also taking Otis for walks on the nearby trails. Otis loved walks, and I wasn't sure if that wasn't part of why he was glad to see me. Although he had a long path ahead to becoming a real dog, he was beginning to see people in a different light.

THE TIE-OUT TECHNIQUE

After Otis settled down about my milling around when he was in his cage and got used to taking treats from my hand, I figured he was relaxed enough to just hang out in my living room. Unfortunately, he immediately became too stressed and again started to pant. I didn't leave him long in that state, because I learned from the previous attempt to give him free run of the house that time alone wasn't going to help. Instead, I put him back in his crate so he could de-stress. I realized that Otis needed some extra help to learn to feel safe outside of a cage, so I used the tie-out technique.

The tie-out is similar to the crate technique except there is no crate. I began Otis's tie-out in a more secluded area and slowly progressed to a less secluded area. What I did with Otis was to first locate him in the corner of my kitchen away from all activity. In this corner, he had two adjoining walls and a nearby kitchen table which limited his exposure to the goings-on in the house. The goal was to find an area that had some seclusion, but where he was not totally hidden away such as under a bed.

I put down a towel for him to lie on. After attaching a six-foot leash onto his collar, the leash was tied to something that would remain secure, even if he suddenly bolted. A tie-out needs to be done to something that won't topple if the dog tries to run off. That halting of a dog who is fleeing in panic can actually reduce the dog's fear. Ironically, allowing a dog to flee would reinforce in the dog's mind that he did need to escape. As long as a dog doesn't feel trapped, stopping a dog from fleeing something that is fearful is helpful. But keep in mind that if you do tether a dog in an area like I did Otis, you need to keep a close watch in case the dog gets tangled.

Having Otis tied in a semi-secluded area allowed him to get used to being out in the house without feeling overwhelmed. At first he was somewhat uneasy about his tie-out area. Fortunately, he wasn't so stressed that he couldn't quit panting like he had when I let him free in the house. While he was tied there, I didn't interact with him. Since he still viewed people as one of his greatest sources of fear, I didn't try to soothe him by occasionally stroking him. If he were not so terrified of all people, I'd have gotten down to his level, talked to him for a few minutes, and perhaps rubbed his chest or worked the area behind the top of his shoulder blades. These areas are well received by shy and uncertain dogs as long as you don't rush things. On the other hand, putting your hand on top of a dog's head is often intimidating.

I gave Otis a few days to learn to get comfortable in his tie-out area. I'd watch for signs that he was beginning to relax a little about this new arrangement. At first, he would try to flee when I passed by. Anytime he did this, I didn't say anything or do anything to him. I just kept a steady gait and didn't pay him any attention. This ignoring rather than paying attention helped him to relax. With dogs who are afraid of people passing by, you need to give them the opportunity to discover that this action is not a threat. If you stop, talk to them, or try to interact by touching them at this point in time, you'll scare the dogs all the more.

When Otis finally became relaxed enough to occasionally nap in his tie-out area, I'd drop him a piece of turkey once in a while. Once he began to move forward to accept that treat from my hand, I felt he was comfortable enough to move him to a less secluded area. I put him on the other side of the kitchen table. There he had a wall behind him, part of a table above him, and a television stand a short distance away. However, there was more area in front of him that was open to my home.

He adapted to this area more quickly. This is typical when working with fearful dogs. Given the chance to conquer their first fear, they begin to learn to relax about something new sooner. With each success, the dog learns more security. Once Otis learned to nap in this new area and move forward for my treats, I released him so he had access to the living room and kitchen. If he hadn't readily adapted to his freedom, I'd have come up with a different area to tie him that was a bit more open than the previous one but not too intimidating. But, after spending time in these two tie-outs, Otis didn't pant when I gave him the run of my kitchen and living room area. He did at first spend a lot of time in the area where he had been tied. Of course, I helped encourage his venturing out by tossing a treat that he had to walk a few steps to get.

Just in case you are wondering if, like Albert, Otis became a pest when I'd lie on the floor while he was off leash, yes he did. While I'd be on the floor, Otis began to come closer to me. He'd lie near me, and I'd reach over to rub his shoulders, his favorite area. Next thing you know, another pest.

Emma Also Needed the Tie-Out Technique

While Emma was at her foster home, Laurel reported that even with her trying to block the area behind the couch, Emma was determined to hide away. The only time Emma came out was at night. Allowing Emma to hide away only increased this dog's sense of insecurity. One day Emma felt so insecure, she began to pee and poop all over the place when Laurel tried to interact with her.

I sent Laurel information on how to use the tie-out technique. This did the trick. Within a week, Emma was beginning to interact with Laurel more like a regular dog. Emma didn't have much time to acclimate to her new braver personality at Laurel's home, because she was soon adopted. Emma did regress in the new home at first, but I instructed the new owners about using the tie-out technique. Emma didn't stay timid long, but learned to relax and to affectionately interact with her new owners.

Why I Fed Turkey

I mentioned that with Otis and Albert, I fed turkey as treats. There were two reasons I did this. The first is that turkey provides a source of nutritious lean meat. Most mill dogs are poorly feed during their lives, and I tried to compensate by feeding high-quality dog food and treats. I like fresh meat bits as treats when I can manage them and prefer to have nitrate-free ones. The second reason was simply that I had turkey left over from our last Thanksgiving meal, making it convenient. If I hadn't had turkey so handy, I'd have used cooked beef or chicken. And since we eat hormone-free meats, so do our foster dogs.

Deciding Among Your Tools

I've given some examples of how I worked to make fearful dogs feel at home as a way of showing you how to use these tools. What you may try if you have a hideaway dog who is not afraid of all people is to lie on the floor for a few hours while watching television and see if the dog comes up to you. If you can't or don't want to lie on the floor, find a place to locate a cage next to where you can sit for a while. Do some reading or watch television while the dog is in the crate nearby. Or you may try tying the dog nearby. You may have to do a little experimenting to find what works best.

IN SUMMARY

Although our goal is to interact with the dog on a personal level, some very fearful dogs need to take that interaction in baby

107

steps. By putting the dog in a crate in an area where you come and go, or using the tie-out technique in an area where you will pass by, the dog can get used to your presence at his own pace. However, if you try to get up close and personal right away, the dog will often feel overwhelmed. If the dog reacts fearfully at first about your presence, try limiting your interactions until he has a chance to acclimate to your home before you ask the dog to feel at ease with you. What you have to realize is that until you create a more trusting relationship with a dog, you will not be able to comfort the dog about his fears. However, by taking your time getting to know the dog, the dog will eventually real- ize you are someone he can feel safe around. But, you must take things at the dog's pace and have a little faith. In the end you will find you can earn the both the dog's trust and affection.

CHAPTER 7

Becoming Your Fearful Dog's Advocate

Don't you just wish you could tell your dog that he or she doesn't need to be afraid? Perhaps you have tried to verbalize that message, but the dog didn't respond the way you'd like. Part of the problem may be the way you are attempting to communicate. Although dogs have a remarkable ability to learn our language, they more often respond to communications we may not be aware we are making. Those communications include our body language and our tone of voice. Dogs also send us messages all the time. By learning how to pick up on a dog's signals, as well as how to use your body language to communicate, you can fast-track a dog's recovery from fear issues.

HOW DOGS UNDERSTAND OUR MESSAGES
When I competed in agility, I learned that dogs can have a different concept about what we think is a clear signal. I'd flip my hand in the direction of a jump and clearly state the word "over," only to have the dog go through a nearby tunnel. Many people who compete in agility begin to learn that dogs often cue off of the direction of their feet and choose that cue over a spoken command or a pointing arm. Competitors learn the quickest way to win ribbons is to change how they give their commands, rather than to train the dog contrary to the dog's natural response.

My second lesson about dog communication happened when I witnessed a woman named Kelly using calming signals to settle down a Boston terrier. Like many brachycephalic breeds (too short of a nose), if the dog gets excited, he can have trouble breathing. Kelly got her dog to calm down enough to catch his breath by using signals he naturally responded to. Other people who have had this problem ended up taking the dog to a vet for drugs to stop the episode. Kelly's "calming signals" worked more immediately.

Kelly told me she learned how to use these signals by reading a book called *On Talking Terms with Dogs: Calming Signals*, written by Turid Rugaas. The book explained how dogs use body language and their eyes to communicate. Although Turid suggested ways to communicate back to dogs using these signals, the greatest value for me when working with fearful dogs was to learn to pick up on some of the dog's signals so I could assess how stressed a dog was feeling. I also learned how not to unintentionally send the wrong message to a fearful dog. I had already experienced that mishap when doing agility.

We all are familiar with the idea that dogs communicate through barking. Over the years, I have noticed that when dogs bark, I can determine what is up by the tone the dog uses and the way the dog barks. A short, rapid bark is an intruder alert. A slow, almost lazy bark is more often heard from a bored dog, while a sharper tone with a similar slower pace is a more demanding dog who may not be content. I've also noticed that dogs respond to our tone of voice, often more specifically than the word we use. If I say a sharp "no," the dog may stop and perhaps cringe. If my "no" is more low and drawn out, the dog will slow and look at me. Your tone of voice can either help a dog feel more secure or less secure. This is an area where a lot of people miscommunicate with their dogs.

There are a lot of books that go into more extensive detail about the communication issues I've mentioned above. In addition to Turid's book on calming signals, there are several books on learning canine body language. All of these are great books to research. In this book, it is my goal to present a mini course on some of the communication you can learn to bring more success when you work with your fearful dog.

LEARNING TO BETTER UNDERSTAND YOUR DOG

In her book *Calming Signals*, Turid points out how dogs communicate with each other through signals. It is important to realize that our dogs are using those same signals to talk to us in a similar nonverbal manner all the time. All we have to do is listen through observation and learn what the dog is trying to tell us. By picking up on this sign language, especially those signals that state how fearful or nervous a dog feels, you can be better prepared to help your dog overcome fears or other behavior issues. Below are some of the signals dogs give and what the dog is trying to tell us with those signals.

Eyes, Head Turns, and Tails

Dogs do a lot of communicating with their eyes. If a dog is staring sharply, the dog may be making a challenge. If the dog looks up at you when he or she is uncertain, the dog is looking to you for guidance. If you stare at an insecure dog, the dog will often divert his or her eyes. That diversion is a way of telling you one of a few things. One is that the dog may feel threatened by your eye contact; another is that the dog feels too uncomfortable with you. Some dogs will divert their eyes to signal that they do not want to challenge you, but are looking for a more peaceful interaction. Dogs whose eyes widen showing white at one side are telling you they are very afraid. Eyes that look like the dog is in pain are often showing fear.

I pay a lot of attention to dogs' eyes because of messages the dog may be sending. Dogs looking away quickly are often signaling me that they are uncomfortable with my presence. I take that as a cue that I need to do something to help them feel more secure. One thing I may do is stop my approach. I typically wait to see if the dog will look back at me. If the dog does, I avoid direct eye contact and work to soften my gaze. I change my approach to less direct. Most dogs view walking towards them in an arc as a friendly gesture.

When approaching a dog, I keep a watch for the dog turning away his head. If a dog turns his head sideways and doesn't look back at me, I may squat down at the dog's level. I like to give a dog a little time without continuing my approach so the dog doesn't feel as threatened. If I were to ignore the dog's message and not temper my approach, the dog would most likely become more insecure or fearful. Sometimes by my halting for a few minutes, the dog has a chance to diffuse some of his fear.

Some other things you may see in a dog's eyes include fear itself. Fear can be a subtle eye widening or a wilder look known as a "whale eye" where you see white on the side. Dogs' eyes may also take on a sharper, more intense look which can appear just before they bite. Often a dog freezes his movements a moment before he strikes.

Dogs can also tuck their tail when uncertain, and some will hunch or curl their backbone as if the eventual goal is to become a ball.

Dominance and Submission

The terms *dominance* and *submission*, as well as *calm submission*, are used frequently when people try to explain dog behavior. These terms are used to label all behavior issues with dogs, leaving the terms with no real significance. Many dog behaviors are a result of a multitude of driving factors. When you are dealing with a very fearful dog, even a dog who is a fear biter, the driving force behind unwanted behaviors has nothing to do with the dog being dominant or needing calm submission.

More on Head Turns

If you read Turid's book on calming signals, you will identify the head turn as a signal a dog uses to try to calm down another dog. I saw Sara, a beagle, do this to Albert. Albert was insecure around dogs he didn't know. When Sara came to meet Albert, he tensed at her approach. She immediately halted and turned her head sideways to send the message "I mean you no harm." This is a common way for one dog to tell another to calm down. I have also used this head-turning technique to send a similar message to a dog who is showing tension when I approach. I stop and turn my head sideways and will give the dog a moment or two to relax. I may even add a yawn to further reassure the dog.

I have often observed mill dogs turn their head sideways to me. But their message is not to calm me down. The dog is telling me he is feeling too much tension at my approach. I have noted that this head turning is more severe than the kind Sara used. Calming head turns are a quarter turn, or sometimes a half turn, and they are not held for a long time. Dogs turning their head because you are scaring them will often make a solid half turn and sometimes more. They may even close their eyes and lower their nose. This is a signal you need to ease off from your approach and give the dog some time to feel less threatened.

Tongue Licking Lips

Tongue licking can have two meanings, just like the head turning. Dogs who are tense but are becoming less tense may lick their lips as a signal they are beginning to relax a little about your interactions. However, more often I see dogs lick their lips as a kind of nervous display, as if they are trying to help themselves settle down a little. Frequently they will need a lot more help to get settled down.

The Guilty Dog Look

Perhaps one of the most misunderstood signals that dogs give us is what many people tag as a guilty look. Dogs displaying this will often lower their head and look at you with what appears to be guilt-filled eyes. Some dogs will either slink away or crawl towards you in a crouched position. You may see this kind of action as the result of scolding the dog, or see it before you've discovered something the dog did that he has seen you get angry about in the past. Sometimes, we may not figure out why the dog is looking guilty. That can be because what we perceive as a guilty look is not actually guilt. This cowering-like action is actually a dog's attempt to soothe us or to show a degree of submission in an attempt to appease us.

Since the dog is not focused on changing his behavior, but instead wants our actions to change, our scolding or disapproval won't change the dog's behavior. All it does is trigger what appears to be a guilty response. The response our dog is giving us is really meant to calm us down. Dogs who feel this level of discomfort in your presence can become all the more insecure, and that insecurity can undermine them getting over their fears.

If you are seeing this kind of a response in your dog, you need to find ways of making the dog feel more comfortable. If you scold or use an angry voice to show disapproval of unwanted behaviors, you need to change that habit. That doesn't mean you need to allow a dog to do things you don't want the dog to do. What it means is that rather than reprimand behaviors you don't like, you need to train for behaviors you do want.

Appeasing behaviors in dogs are cousins to overly submissive behaviors in dogs. Both behaviors undermine confidence in a dog. Dogs who lack confidence can become insecure and fearful. Even after you change the behavior that triggers appeasement behaviors, your dog may need help changing this habit. Chapter four talks about how to change overly submissive habits in dogs. Those same techniques often help dogs stop appeasement behaviors.

Remember, scolding is counterproductive and will not change unwanted behaviors. Learn to teach what you want, rather than punish what you don't want. Punishment is too stressful for some dogs and can perpetuate a sense of insecurity, which can feed fears. You also must not allow overly submissive actions because they can work against you, especially if you have a shyer, more fearful, or very sensitive dog.

AVOIDING BAD CONFRONTATIONS WITH OTHER DOGS

People who have dogs who are afraid of other dogs need to make sure all dog encounters are positive ones. To help keep your dog away from dogs who are unsafe, you need to be able to evaluate the dog's body language when the dog approaches. Don't simply take the owner's word that a dog will be amiable. Learn to watch as a dog approaches to be sure the dog encounter will end positively. If you have any doubts, tell the person your dog is fearful about other dogs and then tell them you'd rather not let your dogs meet. If the approaching dog is not leashed, I will get in between my dog and the other dog.

Some of the behaviors that can alert you that the other dog may not be good for your dog include an erect head, stiffer posture, and raised hackles. Some dogs will become still for a moment and then launch into an attack. Dog owners are well served to watch out for problematic dogs, especially if they have a timid dog. You need to work to make all dog interactions positive to help your dog learn to feel secure.

Actions that are welcomed in dogs include the dog sniffing the ground and approaching indirectly, such as in an arc. These dogs are more likely to result in a good encounter. Keep in mind that many dog owners may not realize their dog has poor social skills. Below is an example of a dog who was not safe to approach, even though the dog owner thought the dog was friendly.

Dogs Wagging Their Tails

Most people think a tail wag is always an announcement of a happy dog. This action is commonly misunderstood because many owners don't know that dogs will wag their tail not only when they are happy, but for other reasons such as if they are stressed or uncertain. To be your dog's advocate, be aware that tail swinging is often done by a tense or nervous dog and is an action that can precede an attack.

I almost had a bad encounter with a dog whose tail wag was not friendly. The owner assured me his off-leash dog was not a threat, but I noticed that the dog had his hackles up, was wagging his tail, and growled as he got close to my dog. I asked the owner if he could take a hold of his dog's collar so his dog didn't scare the timid dog I was training. His owner said, "Don't worry about his growl, he's being friendly." When I asked the owner why he thought his dog was being friendly, the owner stated, "Because he is wagging his tail."

To help determine if an approaching dog is amiable or has bad intentions, don't use tail movement alone to assess the dog's attitude. Instead, practice to identify the signals approaching dogs give as to what is on their mind. Raised hackles are a sign of insecurity. And although some dogs will growl when they are playing, if the dog is approaching your dog and growls, more likely your dog is getting a warning.

Crouching Dogs

As your dog's advocate, always watch out for dogs who crouch as you approach. When a dog crouches, one of two things happens next: Either the crouching dog stands his ground or he attacks. If you see a dog crouch when you approach, stop your approach and step in between your dog and the crouching dog. This can help deflect an attack on your dog.

Blocking

Blocking is when you step in the path of a dog like I did in the examples above. When I block a dog, I square my shoulders and level my head. That secure posture sends an additional message to the dog you are blocking not to try to get past you. Dogs understand this as a signal to back down on an approach. Although this may not deflect a dog who is approaching rapidly, it can be useful for dogs who are less committed to their actions.

Other Canines Encounters to Avoid

Some dogs may be friendly, but can still upset or scare a fearful or reserved dog. Beware of the dog that rushes up to your dog for a greeting. This intense meeting can overwhelm some dogs and leave them intimidated or insecure. Treat the overzealous dog the same way you would any unfriendly dog. Step in the path of that dog and block the encounter. Ask the owner to please not let the dog greet yours.

SHUTDOWN, A SURVIVAL REACTION TO FEAR

Fearful dogs are sending us a lot of communication, and after reading the above examples, I hope you are learning how to better understand your dog's state of mind. Mill dogs, and other highly fearful dogs, can get into fear states beyond what a normal dog experiences. Rather than try to cope, the dog may shut down. By identifying behaviors that signal this kind of state in a dog, you can work to change this counterproductive reaction to fear.

What Is Shutdown?

Dogs who are shut down mentally quit what they are doing and may appear confused. I've seen dogs sometimes do this during

117

competitions like agility if they become stressed when uncertain about what their owner wants. People who work with mill dogs quickly become familiar with the term *shutdown*. Depending on the degree of shutdown in a dog, the dog may merely stop interacting with the owner or completely disassociate with anything in the environment.

Mill dogs can shut down to the degree that they show signs similar to learned helplessness. Learned helplessness is a condition in an animal where the animal has learned to behave helplessly, failing to respond even though there are opportunities for the animal to help itself. Learned helplessness was observed by scientists who placed dogs in a box where the dog received a shock through the floor. At first the dog tried to escape, but found there was no way to escape the shock. Finally the dog would lie down on the floor and give up trying to escape the shock. Later when the dog was put back into the box but given a "safe" area where he would not receive a shock, the dog would not try to avoid the shock by going onto the safe area. Allowing your dog to stay in a helpless state will prevent you from freeing your dog from fear.

The Difference Between Shutdown and Sulking

Sulking is different than the dog shutting down, although some of the dog's actions may appear similar. Sulking is a protest; shutdown is an escape. When a dog sulks, he is protesting something you are doing. I've seen some dogs sulk after I put on a head halter because they didn't like the way the device felt. Such dogs go into a sullen, somewhat pouty state. A sulky dog is showing resentment about something. Although some owners may not like the dog sulking when he is objecting to something the owner just did, the only danger with this kind of action is giving in to it, thus putting the dog in charge.

When the dog shuts down, the dog mentally withdraws from a situation because he cannot cope. This kind of action is a defense mechanism. There are different degrees of shutdown. Some dogs will resist participation in an activity when shutting down. With severe shutdown, the dog escapes by withdrawing mentally and is no longer reacting to stimuli in the environment. A dog in this state has often suffered from extreme or prolonged fear.

Shay Didn't Learn to Quit Pulling, but Merely Shut Down

Shay, a dog mentioned in chapter six, had "shut down" her pulling behavior when she went to a K-9 class for retraining. The trainer used leash corrections to stop the dog's pulling when out on a walk. A leash correction is a hard jerk to stop a dog from pulling or forging ahead on a walk. Instead of learning not to pull, since Shay was so sensitive and fearful, she became stressed over the jerks and shut down her pulling behavior.

Although Shay followed beside whoever held the leash, or slightly behind, she hadn't learned how to heel by responding to cues from the dog handler. The dog had learned to avoid the intolerable leash jerks by moving beside the handler. However, if you looked closely at Shay when she did this, her head was still and her eyes didn't look around at anything in her environment. As well, her gait was not relaxed. She was reacting fearfully when being walked.

As I worked with this dog to become more confident and get over her fears, her leash pulling came back full force. She wanted to move ahead and showed excitement about everything around her. Instead of jerking to stop the pulling, I used a harness where you attach the leash to the chest area. This kind of device helps train dogs not to pull without having to jerk on the dog. Shay finally learned to follow beside me on a loose lead, and eventually without a leash attached.

Head Turning a Shutdown Signal

Although normal dogs will turn their head away to send a calm-ing signal, some dogs who are shutting down may also do this action. There is typically a difference in the way a dog turns his head when sending a calming signal as opposed to shutting down. Dogs who are turning their head to give a calming signal will do a quarter or half turn of their head. That signal will be held for a brief period of time, and the dog will often check back to see if the signal had a positive effect. Dogs will also turn their head to signal you they are feeling too much pressure. A dog that is shutting down when turning his head will do at least a half turn and sometimes more. This extreme head turning, especially when the dog closes his eyes, is an attempt to mentally withdraw from the environment. Dogs in this state will often hunch their shoulders. The dog will keep this position much longer than a calming signal.

This kind of action is not meant to calm you down, but to shut you out. Shutdown like this is a feeble attempt on the dog's part to hide from an unsafe world, a world that is too fearful for the dog to cope in. When you see a dog turning his head in this fashion, take that as a cue that whatever you are doing is causing a lot of stress to the dog. To help out this kind of dog, you need to reduce the stress on the dog. Getting the dog to move forward is one way to help break a shutdown. Try putting a treat right under the dog's nose to lure him into walking for-ward. Use an upbeat tone, but not too excited, to show approval when the dog breaks free of the shutdown.

The Mill Dog Prayer

An extreme form of shutdown is what I call the mill dog prayer. In some mill dog environments, the dogs suffer from prolonged stress all day long. Only at night do the dogs have an opportu-nity to feel less threatened. Some mill dog captives don't appear to have learned how to ever come out of their stressful state during the day.

When stressed mill dogs feel threatened, they tend to go beyond afraid and shut down into what resembles a catatonic state. I've seen mill dogs do this excessive shutdown where they take on a specific posture. I call that posture the mill dog prayer because that is what the dog is appearing to do. The dog will curl his backbone, lower his head, and close his eyes. The dog's muscles are typically tense. This sitting-like position will be kept for quite a while, and often the dog will not come out of this state until you remove what has stressed him or do something to help reduce stress in the dog.

Otis was a champion at this mill dog prayer. He'd quite often go into that prayer mode when we looked at him. He could also manage the prayer when we picked him up and deposited him on a lap for interactions. He'd stay that way the entire time we held him until we realized what was going on. Unfortunately, while he was in this state, what we thought was giving him affection was not getting through. He was shutting us out.

I also encountered this issue in a Chihuahua named Tim I came across at an adoption fair where I'd taken Otis. Otis was hanging out in a pen having some social time with other mill dogs. Meanwhile, several people had stopped by and picked up Tim to cuddle a little with this small, tan dog. I decided to pick up the dog while asking Tim's foster what the story was behind the dog.

Tim had been returned to the rescue after two years because he marked in the house where he'd been adopted. Although this habit could have been corrected, the owner had either not known how to correct the problem or decided not to put in the effort. I was enjoying the way Tim snuggled right down while I held him when it dawned on me he wasn't snuggling at all. I lifted him up and realized his eyes were closed and he was in too tight of a ball to be snuggling. He was in a mill dog prayer.

After two years in a home, he'd never recovered from his fear of people even a little. Tim was not the only dog I encountered who had not overcome his fears from his puppy mill captivity. Although mill dogs can become as relaxed as other dogs, they need help to do so.

Albert not only did a mill dog prayer, but had a second way he'd shut down. He'd curl into more of a ball and not be able to sit at all when he went into this catatonic-like state. His uncomfortable position made his distress easier to identify. He'd stay in that ball until he felt less afraid. Although these dogs suffered from excessive fear, both Otis and Albert made a full recovery.

If you have a dog who is shutting down, one thing to try is to do the soothing touch to systematically unlock the dog from that catatonic-like state. At first, that was what helped Otis. As he became more at ease with me, I'd put a piece of turkey under his nose to try to get him to eat. If that didn't work, I'd make a clicking noise with my tongue. This would get him to turn his attention my way. Then, I'd work to get him to take a step forward. A dog moving forward helps him leave his fear behind.

CHAPTER 8

Establishing a Foundation of Security in Your Dog

Fear is your dog's enemy. However, a lot of people have dogs who may really love them but don't trust their owner when afraid. With no trust, it is hard for the dog to feel secure or to be reassured by their owner. That fear needs to be replaced with a confident relationship between dog and owner. Using a method called the soothing touch is one way to teach a dog not to be afraid. Establishing yourself as a confident leader to your dog is another way to help build confidence in a dog. Sometimes a dog owner will need to desensitize the dog to specific issues to help free the dog from fear. These are the topics contained in this and the next two chapters.

BUILDING CONFIDENCE IN A DOG WITH TOUCH

Some dogs love pets and attention but seem to become unsettled when touched on certain parts of their body. When touched, those areas are like pockets of fear that can bring uncertainty in the relationship between dog and owner. Those pockets of fear are areas of tension dogs have in their body when they are uncertain. Unfortunately, some dogs are constantly tense, which doesn't allow them to ever seem to feel secure. To determine if a dog has pockets of fear or a lack of trust about being handled, you need to make sure the dog is comfortable being touched on every part of his body.

I learned a lot about the benefits of using touch to desensitize all areas of an animal many years ago. Before I worked with dog issues, I worked with problematic horses. The idea of resolving fear issues in the animal was matter-of-fact. Touching the animal in a reassuring way was used to build a level of confidence between me and the horse. By first teaching a horse to become comfortable when touched all over, I found it easier to put on saddles and to reassure the horse when afraid. When I transitioned to working with dogs, like many trainers, I used food and other positive motivators to help desensitize dogs to things that scared them. However, after working with highly fearful dogs, I have discovered that teaching a dog to accept touching all over has a settling effect similar to what I witnessed in horses. That effect is that the animal learns to calm down. This method is far superior to simply using food to desensitize the dog.

Many dog owners live with dogs who become very upset if the owner touches certain areas on them. Those areas of tension become a blockade for a dog when it comes to trusting his owner. Even after the dog is comfortable with being touched all over, the dog needs to learn to relax when tense. Just as people hold tension in certain parts of their body when they feel stressed, so do dogs. By working to diffuse tense areas on a dog's body, you'll have a better chance of the dog learning to relax when uncertain.

GOOD "FIRST CONTACT" AREAS ON DOGS

There are two areas that you will have better luck with when making first contact with a fearful dog. One is the chest, and the other is the area on the dog's back just behind the shoulder blades. Albert preferred the chest as the first place of contact, and Otis preferred the area behind his shoulder blades. Many dogs find rubbing in these areas soothing, and that feeling can help relax them.

124

How I choose which area to start with depends on how the dog reacts. I first try the area behind the shoulder blades. If the dog shows discomfort or avoids my reach, I approach the chest. Once the dog becomes comfortable with the chest, I work my way through soothing touches to the area behind the shoulder blades. That area typically becomes the "home base" for the dog.

WHERE THE SOOTHING TOUCH CAME FROM

In 1971 I read an article in a horse magazine describing a technique used by Dr. William Linfoot. The article described how this DVM could calm a wild horse in one hour. A lot of his technique involved using touch to soothe the animal. Within a few months of reading this article, I had the opportunity to use the technique on a two-year-old untamed horse who was highly fearful of people. Although it took me a week to accomplish what Dr. Linfoot did in an hour, I learned a lot through that experience and found many ways to employ this technique over the years when working horses with fear issues.

Ironically, over twenty years ago when I changed from working with problematic horses to working with problematic dogs, I didn't at first use this technique. Many dogs have a working relationship with people, and Dr. Linfoot's technique is geared towards animals that do not have a history of contact with humans. That was why Linfoot chose to work with wild horses when using the technique. He found they were better candidates than ones who'd become fearful of people through abuse.

With the pet dogs, I approached the dog's fear issues by tapping into the dog's established training and trust, or by creating or expanding trust through training. However, many years ago I was walking an insecure foster who reacted fearfully when a dog rushed up to a fence and barked at her. I found myself adapting part of Linfoot's technique on the dog to settle her down, and it worked well. When I encountered Otis and Albert, who were both fear biters, I quickly realized that to solve their biting issues, I needed to solve their fear about people handling them.

Having worked so many years using parts of Linfoot's technique with highly fearful horses, my hands seemed to know just how to succeed with dogs. I called what I did with these dogs the "soothing touch." I have since used this technique on a lot of fearful dogs and found it helps teach the dogs to learn to feel more secure with their owners when the dogs are in a fearful situation. Working to get a dog to feel completely relaxed with an owner, no matter where the owner touches the dog, helps build trust and confidence between dog and owner. After all, a lot of times when our dogs are fearful, all we need is for the dog to trust us and relax.

USING THE SOOTHING TOUCH

Before you attempt to do the soothing touch on a dog, first practice on yourself or someone else. Put your three middle fingers on one spot on your scalp with about a quarter- to half-inch gap between each finger. The position should feel comfortable to you. Anchor your fingers by placing your thumb on your head in a position that feels comfortable and natural. When practicing on the scalp area to learn this technique, first move your fingers back and forth, then move them in a small circle on your scalp without picking up the tips or moving from the contact area.

You are practicing on your head because there is no muscle to indent or apply too much pressure. This technique is not a muscle massage, and too much or too little pressure will not get you the results you want. What you are striving for is movement of the skin over the muscle, making light contact with the muscle, which creates a soothing feeling. I suggest using the scalp so

126

you learn not to press too hard when using this technique. When you have muscle below, if you apply too much pressure, the feeling is not comforting, thus this training is giving your fingers an opportunity to learn what is and is not a good pressure when you work on the dog where there will be muscle below.

If you know people who like scalp massages, you can practice on them. They can tell you if you are using the right pressure. However, keep in mind that the right pressure will vary with different people as it will with different dogs. The pressure will also vary with the amount of tension in the individual. So don't hesitate to hone your skills by working with different people, especially if they have had successful scalp massages and can give you good feedback.

When I do this with a dog, the dog's tension directs how the process proceeds. On small dogs, I often find myself beginning with my fingertips. With larger dogs, I use more of the finger pad. Dogs have much looser skin than people, which allows the opportunity to make bigger circles without lifting and moving your fingers. However, just because you can make bigger circles on a dog doesn't mean you want to. Often, when working a very tense dog, you may find yourself only moving your fingertips back and forth until the dog beings to relax in that area. As the dog relaxes, begin to do small circles.

This technique does not involve moving the fingers over the surface of the dog's skin, but is done by moving the dog's skin over the muscle using the right amount of contact to give a soothing and calming effect. The direction of the circle depends on what the dog responds best to, which you can discover by doing a little experimenting. If the dog doesn't respond to your attempts to do the soothing touch no matter which direction you move in a circle, experiment with the pressure by increasing or decreasing it a little. Go at a relaxed and calming pace. Faster movements reflect the dog's tension, but do not help to release it. Keep in mind that for the dog to relax, you must communicate that you are relaxed and secure.

With dogs who are used to people, I often move easily over relaxed areas only to find areas of tension that take more effort to work through. I am never in a hurry when doing this, but spend the time needed on each area to get the dog to relax. Be aware that some dogs may not be extremely tense in all areas. However, if the dog is a little tense, the dog will benefit by getting him to completely relax. You need to find and resolve any area and degree of tension.

Many of my soothing touch sessions are done for about half an hour. On occasion, I've done more time or less time. I seldom get all the results the dog needs in one session. Typically dogs need several sessions to learn to relax tension all over the body. The progress becomes what it needs to be for each dog. Even though I am very experienced in working with tense animals using this technique, I can only get as far as the dog can go in each session, and no two dogs are alike. However, doing a session a day will help even the most tense dog improve.

ESTABLISHING HOME BASE

I like to establish what I call a "home base" on a dog. This is an area that the dog finds very comforting, where the dog can more quickly relax when worked, even if he is feeling tense. I find one of the most secure areas to establish home base is the area behind the shoulder blades at the top of the back. I begin working the dog behind the shoulder blades and stay there until the dog learns to completely relax about that area.

Sometimes a dog who is not settling down very well when first worked at home base will benefit by rubbing the chest area at the same time that home base is worked. Once the dog learns to settle down doing both areas, transition to only doing the area behind the shoulder blades at the top of the back. Don't hesitate to do a little experimenting.

USING THE WORD "EASY" TO CUE THE DOG

I use a cue word to help the dog learn to relax. I typically introduce this cue word early in my rubbing process, shortly after I established home base. My favorite word to use is "easy" since I've used that word on horses for so many years, but you can use a different word if you prefer. When taught correctly, you will find the word alone will help a dog begin to relax, even before you return to work at home base to reinforce the word.

To teach the dog the "easy" cue, sit the dog on your lap, or if you have a larger dog, find a way to comfortably work the dog at home base. You can also put a larger dog on a grooming table if you have one. Rub home base while saying "easy." Your tone of voice is important. You are not trying to motivate or reprimand the dog. Your voice needs to reflect your goal, which is to calm the dog. The best tone is a calm and soothing one.

Once the dog relaxes, go to an adjoining place to rub. If the dog tenses, immediately respond to that tension by saying your soothing "easy," then go right to home base and work until the dog relaxes. Say the word "easy" a few times while working at home base. Make sure the dog completely relaxes while you are saying the word and working at home base.

Once the dog is completely relaxed, you can again go back to the area where the dog tensed and work for a moment or two. If the dog begins to relax on that second visit, use the word "easy" to reinforce that he relaxed just like the word asked him to. Don't forget to reinforce that experience by returning to home base and soothing him there while telling him "easy." This helps in the process of teaching the dog that when he hears the word "easy," he can expect to relax.

After teaching the word "easy," you may find a dog responds to the word so well that you don't need to go back to home base. Just be sure to keep rubbing that area after you use the word until the dog completely settles down. "Easy" needs to become synonymous with complete relaxation.

WORKING PATTERNS FOR THE SOOTHING TOUCH

Once I have success with the dog relaxing when I work home base and have introduced the word "easy," I begin to venture out on the dog's body. Typically the first place I venture to is the dog's shoulder area, behind the point of the shoulder and above the elbow of the dog. I slowly venture into that area, and although there is a lot of muscle, I do not massage the area. The soothing touch is not a massage. I keep my pressure at a point where I work the very surface of the muscle in a soothing way. What makes that touch soothing is the response the dog gives me. I learn information about how the dog responds when I establish home base. Establishing home base tells me a lot about what kind of pressure is needed to get the dog to relax.

I don't have a time expectation when working, but take whatever time needed to reach the goal of the dog relaxing in each area. After I work successfully on the shoulder, I don't move on to the leg area below. With a lot of dogs, legs and especially the feet can take more work, so I first secure other areas before doing those.

The next area I typically work is down the back. But I don't jump from the shoulder to the backbone. Instead, I use those soothing strokes to make my way back to home base. I work there for a short bit of time to reinforce relaxation. I often repeat "easy" while I work at home base to remind the dog what the cue word means. Typically I use more of my fingertip on the backbone area and work small areas as I gradually make progress.

Once the dog feels nice and relaxed, I work my fingers down the back, working the area on both sides of the backbone at the same time. Often this means using my thumb and middle finger. I take my time on this path because a lot of dogs can have a lot of tension along their spine when they are insecure. That is why you see dogs curl their spine when afraid. If a dog's body begins to grow tense while I work down the backbone, I will say the

130

word "easy" and linger at that tense area, working to dispel the tension before returning to home base to get the dog to fully relax. I repeat "easy" to mark that relaxation at home base, then work my way back to the tense area. I use soothing strokes as I travel, rather than pick up my fingers and move from one area to the next.

Once I work down to the base of the tail, I spend some time there. How long depends on the dog. A lot of dogs find working this area is soothing, while others don't respond as much. If the dog's tail is clamped, I lift it gently upward, then let it go. I often do this three or four times until the tail begins float rather than clamp back down. If the dog can't keep from clamping his tail, I return to home base and rework the spine beginning from home base to the tail. I'll do it a third time if needed, then I'll work for a while at home base and quit for the day. The next day, after I work at home base, I then work the areas where I had success before I go back to the challenging area. I don't move on until this area is conquered. Once the tail is unclamped, I work on the tail itself, working to seek out and loosen up any tight muscles.

The next area I like to work is the neck and head. Of course, I begin by first working home base. When it comes time to working the ears, if the dog likes that a lot, I will sometimes rub that area until the dog relaxes, then quit the session. Before I call this area done, I work all over the head, including between the eyes and the muzzle. I don't try to lift the lips until later, after I've gotten the entire dog's body relaxed.

When I'm ready to work the legs, I work first at home base. Then I again work the shoulder, as if applying an extra coating of relaxation. Slowly I work down the leg to the top of the front foot. With some dogs who are touchy about the feet, if I have worked the dog successfully up to that point, I may not go all the way to home base. Some dogs will learn to accept your touching the feet if you work there a moment, then go to the

131

shoulder and work that area, then go back to working feet. Don't work a little on each foot; instead, conquer each foot one at a time. At least you need to touch the entire top of the foot and pick up and hold the paw. If the dog has a lot of difficulty with this, work to get the dog to relax before you end the session. Take however many days it takes to get the dog to relax about contact with his foot.

Some dogs may pull away when you first touch the top of the foot. If the dog pulls his foot away, say "easy" but don't remove your hand. Wait until the dog sets down his foot, then amiably go to the closest area where you can rub the dog and have success, such as the shoulder. Rub until the dog relaxes, then again work down towards the foot. Work slowly but steadily to touch the top of the foot. If you feel the dog tense prior to your reaching the foot, say "easy" then work the area of tension until the dog relaxes. If this diffusing of tension takes a while, visit home base and reemphasize the word "easy. " Revisit the tense area and make sure that area has learned to relax before venturing farther down the foot.

When you do go to pick up and hold the foot, if the dog tries to pull away, don't immediately let go. It is okay to resist the dog jerking his foot, as long as the dog doesn't panic. Once the dog gets comfortable with you holding his foot, you can begin your digit work.

Conquer one digit at a time. Only move on to the next digit when you secure the previous one. Don't forget to work one foot at a time until that entire foot is yours to handle as you want. Work each toe on each foot, remembering to get the dog to totally relax afterwards. Often this means visiting home base. Finally, you will be able to hold the foot as if you were going to clip the toenails. (Toenail clipping is covered in chapter ten.)

TENSION LEVELS IN DIFFERENT DOGS

When I work with highly fearful dogs who are not used to positive handing from people, it is fairly easy to feel the dog's tension in the muscles. However, with dogs who are more used to human touch, I am able to go over a lot of the dog's body without finding a lot of tension. I still cover every square inch. Sometimes I've noticed that even though the dog doesn't show a lot of tension in his body, he is still a little tense or I discover an area the dog doesn't like touched. That tension needs to be worked out and areas of resistance need to be changed to ones where the dog doesn't mind being touched.

One thing that can cause tension in an otherwise comfortable dog is when you are doing something that concerns the dog. For example, if you take your dog to the veterinarian, the dog may feel tenser than if he is accompanying you to the PetSmart. Dogs often signal us that they are insecure with body language. Some may lag behind rather than walk in a carefree manner. The dog's tail may lower and the eyes take on a concerned look. In these kinds of situations, I can then find tension in areas on the dog where there was not tension before. I work using the soothing touch with these dogs to help them learn to relax about the little things that upset them. By working out mild tension, you can often see the dog's confidence and sense of relaxation improve.

HIDDEN FEARS THAT GROW INTO ISSUES

The soothing touch is a great way to not only help dogs feel more relaxed and secure, but also desensitize fear in them. The sooner you eliminate fear, the better. Fear that isn't resolved can sometimes take root and grow. Below is a hypothetical scenario to illustrate these points.

A dog is often put on a grooming table for brushing. The first time this particular dog was up on the table, the dog felt a bit uncertain. However, since brushing the dog is a soothing experience, after a few times, the dog didn't mind this process. Then one day the owner decided to do what is called a sanitation clip on the dog. The owner used some electric clippers and shaved the hair below the dog's tail to prevent any feces from sticking to hair in that area. This owner didn't desensitize the dog to the clippers (desensitizing is talked about in chapter ten) but merely went to work on the task. The dog was nervous about this process, but the owner got the task done.

The next time the owner put the dog on the grooming table, the dog was a little tense. From here, there are several ways this can play out. First, since the owner won't do another sanitation clip for several more visits to the grooming table, the dog can again learn to relax about being on the table if the dog finds the grooming process relaxing. That sense of relaxation can make the dog less apprehensive the next time the owner does a sanitation clip, and finally, the dog may quit fretting about being clipped.

Another possibility is that the dog gets tenser every time the owner goes to groom the dog after the clipper incident. The next time the owner turns on those clippers, the dog begins to fight about the clippers being used. If the owner does anything adverse to the dog when this happens, that action only convinces the dog that this situation is one to fear, which can trigger a fight-or-flight reaction. Soon even brushing becomes a fight, or even the dog being touched.

The best scenario is that the owner realizes the dog reacted with more tension than expected about the clippers. Since this dog shows a lot of tension about being clipped, the owner can now work to reverse the damage using the soothing touch. To do this, the owner would put the dog on the table the day after the clippers incident. The owner would begin to check for tension areas in the dog's muscles. A good way to do this is to begin at home base, and work all over the dog as described in the section that talks about working patterns for the soothing touch. The owner would work out any tense areas. Once that was accomplished, the owner would end the session.

The next day the owner would again put the dog on the table and work out any tense areas. If this goes well, the owner would brush the dog for a short time, then recheck for tension. Some dogs who become afraid will associate the brushing with a possible frightening event. To be safe, the owner needs to make sure the dog remembers that brushing is a positive experience. This process would be continued until the dog no longer showed tension about being brushed on the grooming table. Before the owner again uses the clippers, the owner would do some desensitization using a technique similar to the one used for dogs having their nails clipped. The owner would be best served to separate the desensitization work from brushing the dog.

A FEW COMMENTS ON THE SOOTHING TOUCH

Mistakes I've Seen People Make
One of the common mistakes people make when trying to use this technique on their dog is instead of working at a steady, soothing pace when their dog tenses, they often speed up their movement, and I suspect they unintentionally press down harder. This unintended action can increase tension in the dog.

Bonding
Since doing this kind of touch can double as a bonding exercise, don't hesitate to work on your dog anytime you sit down to relax with your pet.

Working Pet Dogs
When working with pet dogs that normally are not holding a lot of fear and tension in their muscles, I find myself using a different approach than with highly fearful dogs. I can sometimes stroke along some of the muscles looking for tension areas when the dog doesn't have a lot of muscle tension all over the body. This speeds up my efforts to find and work on the problem areas.

The Truth about How I Do This Technique

I tried to describe how I use this on dogs, but in all honesty, I have more experience on horses—my fingers just know what to do, how much to do, and how to pace things without any conscious thought. My recommendation for dog owners using this technique is to remember you are learning as well as teaching, so give yourself time and be patient, consistent, and calm when working your dog. Don't be afraid to experiment, and always work at your dog's pace.

CHAPTER 9

Fighting the War on Fear through Leadership

Dogs want their owners to be their leader. Taking that role earns you the dog's love and loyalty. If your dog is insecure, seeing you as a strong leader will build security in the dog. Ironically, our dogs want from us a lot of the same kind of leadership we desire from a strong leader. We want our leaders to be in charge of things and provide guidance, as well as tackle challenges with a stable approach and a calm demeanor. We expect our leaders to help us navigate in areas where we don't know the rules. As a human leader, we need to go beyond normal dog culture and teach the dog appropriate behaviors in our society.

These days, some people confuse being their dog's leader with taking on an alpha role. Behind this concept is the notion that dogs are like wolves. The truth of the matter is that dogs are so diverse in their behaviors from selective breeding for specific traits that you will find a diversity of behaviors in dogs. Most of those behaviors don't reflect much of the dog's wolf heritage.

In general, dogs don't want you to assume the role of an alpha or what you perceive as an alpha. Although some group dynamics exist between you and your dog, they have little to do with the human in an alpha position. Dogs are bred to allow people to train them in how we want them to behave. Most dogs do poorly if their owners try to force or attempt to bully them into compliance. Two key factors in establishing leadership that builds confidence in the dog are to use positive techniques and to eliminate any behaviors and interactions that work against confidence in a dog.

TRAINING YOUR DOG

A lot of people teach their dogs to sit and stay. Teaching the basics using positive techniques is a good start, because training sets up communication that eliminates the culture gap between dog and human. Training also establishes compliance in the dog. However, basic training is only part of the journey. To complete the kind of training that helps your dog see you as a leader, you need to train the dog to relinquish possessions and to look to you for guidance. As well, some dogs will need to be trained on impulse control.

This chapter will touch on some of the training all dogs need to establish the owner's leadership role. Some dogs with specialized drives bred into them, such as a strong guarding drive, may require additional training to help the dog know how to appropriately react when internal urges would have them take actions contrary to their owner's desires.

VOICE IS A TOOL

These days, many people train dogs armed with treats. However, another more readily available tool is your voice. I've given examples about the right way and wrong way to use your voice in a few of the previous chapters. I'd now like to address this training tool more formally.

How you use this tool will vary with each dog. Some dogs respond quite readily to a stern tone of voice, and that tone can stop unwanted behaviors. Sensitive dogs may overreact to a stern tone. An overreaction to any kind of reprimand leaves the dog focusing on the reprimand and not the action you want the dog to stop.

In general:

- A bright, motivational tone will encourage and reward a dog.

- A calmer voice can help reassure a dog who is uncertain.

- A stern tone will often make a dog stop an unwanted behavior.

When using a stern tone with your dog, make sure the dog reacts in the appropriate way. If the dog is a more sensitive dog, a stern or harsh tone can cause the dog to wince as if you struck him or to become afraid of you. With some sensitive dogs, you may not be able to use a stern tone at all.

A frantic or too chipper/fake voice will stress a dog or excite the dog. Sometimes that tone can trigger a predatory response, which is why some dogs will chase a kid who is running and screaming.

BASIC TRAINING TO ESTABLISH COMMUNICATION

Sit

A common way to teach a dog this command is to say the word "sit" and then use a treat to lure the dog into the right position. You can do this by showing the dog the treat, stating the command, then moving the treat from the dog's nose over the top of his head at a pace that allows the dog to follow the treat. Once the dog's behind lands on the ground, you can say "good sit" and give the reward.

The reason to verbally acknowledge the right behavior rather than just hand over the treat is that a verbal acknowledgment is a quicker way to tell the dog the exact moment the task was done right. Some dogs may pop out of the sit while trying to eat the treat and may not as quickly make the right association.

Teaching a Mill Dog to Sit

When I first worked with some of the mill dogs, they were fairly insecure about taking a treat from me. At best, they would take a step forward to eat a treat. However, moving that treat in an attempt to lure the dog would often cause the dog to abandon accepting the treat. The dog was simply too uncertain about my actions to follow a treat into a sitting position.

The technique I used instead was to capture the behavior I wanted by acknowledging that behavior using a command, then tossing the treat. To do that, I had a high-value treat at the ready. When the dog sat down nearby, I'd say "sit" and then toss the treat. I'd let the dog take his time going to retrieve the treat, and if needed, I'd walk off in the beginning, since the tossing action by me was a bit intimidating for some of the more insecure dogs. After we had been doing this for a while, the dog would sometimes glance at me and sit. I'd tell the dog "good sit" and reward. When the dog began to sit more often, I'd work to say the command when the dog looked at me so I could get the command stated before the dog sat. After a few successes, the dog learned how to sit on command. I was slow at fading the treat.

Fading a Treat

Treats are great when training to give the dog a positive association with what you are training the dog to do, as well as to motivate the dog to do the command. Ideally, once the dog understands the command, you begin to fade the treat. You do this by offering the treat every other time, then every third or fourth time. Praise can be given intermittently to keep the dog encouraged. Soon you don't need to use a treat at all: The dog understands the command and has the habit of complying.

With dogs who are reluctant to comply, you may need to occasionally give a treat reward to keep up the motivation. With fearful dogs, I tend to reward longer than with other dogs and don't stop until the dog becomes very comfortable doing the command. However, some people neglect fading the treat. This is a bad idea. Dogs who will not do a task unless you first offer a reward see themselves in charge. Some dogs even blackmail their owners with the attitude of no treat, no compliance. That diminishes the dog's view of you as a strong leader. Dogs need to learn to follow your command because you are the leader, not because you are bribing them with a treat.

Down or Lie Down
This term is often misused by people. They tell a dog "down" to lie down, but also tell the dog "down" when they want the dog to get off the couch or stop jumping on them. A better term for the latter is "off." Dogs benefit when we use consistent terms.

To teach a dog to lie down, you do it very similar to the sit command. Using a treat, you say the command, then lure the dog into the desired position. With more timid dogs like mill dogs, you can capture the correct behavior in the same way you did the sit command. If your dog has a hard time being lured into a down position—I've seen this with some corgis—don't hesitate to use this technique to capture the desired behavior.

The Long Down Stay
About twenty years ago, a dog trainer in a class I attended introduced me to the importance of having a dog in the down position and for the dog to learn to stay there until you release the dog. He worked with a lot of northern breeds such as malamutes and also helped with wolf dog rescues. His approach was to force the dog into a down position. If the dog tried to get up, the dog was shoved back down and made to comply. The

trainer was both right and wrong. He was right about the value of a long down stay, but wrong in his approach.

Training a dog to do a long down stay on command begins to build you as a leader. The dog learns to comply for more than a moment. Some dogs get into the habit of offering a token compliance. The dog lies down for a moment, then gets up wanting a reward. That kind of behavior doesn't create the kind of respect you need from a dog who sees you as a strong leader. A dog needs to respect your command for as long as you say. I've seen this issue in hard-to-train dogs, including more independent dogs and pushy dogs.

I've found several benefits to teaching more problematic dogs the long down stay. Dogs who seem to have a hard time following their owner's commands, who are stronger-willed or pushy, benefit from practicing a long down stay. When the dog has to do a command for a longer period of time, the dog has the opportunity to focus more on the owner, rather than having the attitude he is manipulating the owner for a reward. Another benefit for some dogs is that teaching them to do a long down stay can help create a more calm and secure dog. The dog's attention on doing the command seems to help the dog forget any angst he may be feeling. I've seen a long down stay help dogs who tend to whine a lot around their owners. The long down stay teaches the dog to focus on the task rather than continually vocalize his uncertainty.

Teaching the Long Down Stay

My favorite way to teach a long down stay is to reward the down stay while the dog is doing the task, rather than reward after the task is complete. To do that, ask the dog to lie down, then say "stay." As soon as you give the stay command, give him a treat. Wait a moment, then again say "stay" and give another treat. This way you are rewarding the actual act of staying, not the point where the dog no longer does the command.

Do about five treat rewards in a row, hesitating a few moments between each reward. At first, repeat the stay command with each treat. If the dog happens to pop out of the down stay, don't worry. Simply ask the dog to lie back down and continue rewarding the behavior you want the dog to do. When you are done asking the dog to stay, give a release word such as "okay" or "free." Walk a few steps away to encourage the dog to get up, but don't give any rewards for the dog ending the down stay. In a few minutes, repeat the exercise. Do this training a few times in a row, then take a few hours break and repeat. Try to do at least two or three practices the first day.

If your training went well the first day, add a bit more time between the command and the reward. As before, if the dog breaks the stay, don't reprimand, just place the dog back into the stay position. Slowly work up to fewer rewards as well as more time staying. If the dog seems to have a hard time doing this task, don't move on to the next part of the training. Instead, repeat the lesson the next day. Only progress to the next part of the training once the dog does well in a training session. Eventually, the dog will begin to have better success in the training, and you can do more training sessions in one day, with a break in between each training session.

After a few practice sessions, your dog should be fine about staying on command for a minute with only one or two rewards. When the dog reaches this point, say "stay" and take a step away. Come right back, repeat the stay command, and reward. Work at the dog's pace to take a few more steps away in each practice session. Soon you can work up to walking around while the dog is lying down nearby for two or three minutes, with the dog only getting an occasional reward. Remember to give a release command when you are done. Don't reward when you release the dog, either verbally or with a treat, just calmly walk away. The goal is to get the dog to focus on the stay and understand that the stay is rewarded. This

143

helps motivate the dog to do this more willingly, as well as not to anticipate a reward once the task is complete.

Typically each training practice is done successfully one time before you take a break. When you take a break, allow at least an hour in between practices as long as the dog readily succeeds with the next training. If the dog stalls out on his progress, try adding more time in between training sessions or trying the training the next day. Only do several training sessions in one day if the dog progresses well. If you only do this a couple of times a day, you can still meet your goal.

The Come Command

There are a lot of ways to teach the come command and a lot of rules to making this command work. The easiest way to begin to teach the come command is to take out a treat and say "come" when the dog arrives, then give the dog the treat. A rule to preserve a good come command is to never call the dog over to scold or punish him, or any other adverse action. Nevertheless, there are other things that can weaken a come command, including allowing a dog to "blow you off" about the command. If you allow a dog to dawdle when you call the dog to come, responding to that command only when the dog feels like it, you lose some of the respect the dog has for you as a leader. A loss of respect in this fashion makes a dog less secure about you when the dog feels threatened.

If your dog is preoccupied doing his thing rather than complying, you can quietly walk over, take hold of the dog's collar, and help the dog to comply. Once you arrive to where you first called the dog, have the dog sit and ask the dog to stay. Take a few steps backwards and call the dog to you using the come command. Reward the compliance. This exercise is used to emphasize to your dog that as a strong leader, you don't allow the dog to ignore your commands. However, be aware that some dogs merely need to have more motivation to respond to your request. Before using insistence to help sharpen up their come response, try using some of the motivational techniques talked about below.

Teaching a Mill Dog to Come before He Got Over His Fear of Me

Albert was more willing from the beginning to take treats. Otis, if your arm wasn't outstretched to the fullest and your head turned sideways, wouldn't consider the piece of turkey held out, at least at first. Often I had to drop the treat, then move away for him to eat it. Since Albert was more willing to come forward, he was the first one taught to come on command. He learned this before he was comfortable with me picking him up.

To teach Albert to come, the word "come" was stated, then a treat was given. After giving a treat a few times when "come" was said, Albert was asked to take a step forward to get the treat. Over time, he worked up to more and more steps for the treat. Once he became comfortable with coming on command, I began to say "come, come, come" in a bright and motivational tone. Albert appeared to like that tone a lot, and he'd meet me at the front of his cage to get a treat. Before long, the come command could be chanted, and he'd follow all the way outside for his morning potty time. Albert seemed to love the "come" chant because he liked upbeat tones.

One day, when I was in a back bedroom, I called his name and chanted "come, come, come" in my usual motivation tone. He didn't come. I began looking for him only to discover the front door had blown open. Frantic, I went outside to search for him on the acre around our house. He wasn't there. I walked down my driveway and began to go down the street where we'd walked together in the past. There he was alongside the dirt road, appearing to be searching for me. I called in that "come" chant and he came running to me, then followed me into the house. At this point in his training, he was still uncertain about me reaching to pick him up. Without that reliable come command, he'd have been one hard dog to catch.

Adding Motivation to a Come Command

With the come command being so important, it is a good idea to add motivation anytime you can. Although Albert found my chant motivating, other dogs may respond to different kinds of motivations. One way to encourage a dog to like coming is to call the dog to come towards you before you unsnap a leash to let the dog run and play. This may require your taking a step or two backwards, but this can set in the dog's mind that come is associated with getting to play, not just ending playtime. If you have a dog that loves playing with a toy or ball, pick up that item and call the dog to come when you plan on playing with him. This will create a lot of motivation in the dog to come running when you call. You may want to do this intentionally for a while until the dog shows strong enthusiasm whenever you call him to come.

TRAINING TO BUILD MORE LEADERSHIP

Dogs expect a leader to control the resources. What that means is all those dog toys don't belong to your dog, nor do any of those chew bones. They belong to you. But since you love your dog, you allow the dog to play with or chew those items. If you allow your dog to own them, the dog will probably not allow you to take them away anytime you want or need to. Dogs who feel they own toys or chew bones will sometimes fight other dogs over those items.

Allowing your dog to feel as if he owns possessions in the house, including the bed he sleeps on, weakens your position as a leader in the dog's perspective. To strengthen your position as a leader, you need to teach the dog to give up any item in his possession on command. That training puts you in control of when the dog gets items (food, bed, treats, toys) and lets you set the rules for sharing of resources.

The Pitfall of Overindulging a Dog

It is easy to want to spoil our beloved companions. Unfortunately, spoiling a dog will undermine a dog's sense of security. We all love indulging our dogs, but we shortchange a dog by not giving the dog the structure provided by training and leadership. Our dogs are under our charge, and we owe them a sound and secure home. Dogs who have this kind of home are more secure and have a closer bond with their owners.

DOGS LOOKING FOR GUIDANCE

Dogs who see their owners as strong leaders will look to their owners for guidance. That literally means the dog learns to look at the owner. A dog who looks to an owner for guidance is good. Unfortunately, dogs with more impulsive tendencies will act without any guidance from the owner. When this is not corrected, the dog begins to lose respect for the owner as a leader. (Corrected means the owner insists the dog do the command correctly, but doesn't punish the dog.) Dogs who have this problem often need to learn impulse control.

It is important to teach your dog to seek your guidance before taking certain actions. Training a dog in this manner puts you in a stronger leadership role. The training used to accomplish this is called the watch command.

The Watch Command

I teach the watch command two different ways. The first way is to say "watch" and then take a treat and raise it to your eyes. Once the dog looks at your eyes, hand over that treat. The other way is to teach the dog to look at you before acting impulsively. The second way helps dogs who are a bit more willful or who are having problems always complying with an owner's commands.

To teach the dog the watch command the second way, first ask the dog to sit. Then hold the treat out sideways by extending your arm. Dogs often look at the treat in your hand and not at your eyes. Wait until the dog happens to glance away from the treat for a moment. When the dog does this, say "good" and then reward with a treat.

Once again, hold out the treat and wait. Typically the dog looks away sooner. Again the word "good" tells the dog the moment something was done correctly, and the treat becomes the prize. After doing this a few times, the dog often begins to look right at you when you hold the treat to the side. At that point, use the word "okay" to mark the desired behavior. This is a good time to award a jackpot of several treats at a time and end the first lesson.

After about an hour or so, you can repeat the lesson. Before the training is complete, switch which hand holds the treat. This teaches the dog that when he wants something to look to you. This also sets up for additional training to help more willful or impulsive dogs, including the leave-it command.

What Is a Jackpot?

A regular reward is typically one treat to support a particular action. A jackpot is when you give several treats as a bonus. This tells the dog that the action was done exactly the way you wanted it done.

GROWING YOUR LEADERSHIP STATUS

Training drop-it, leave-it, impulse control, relinquishing posses-sion, and moving a dog from a sleeping area helps to put the dog owner in charge of the resources. Dogs expect the leader to control the resources. Accomplishing this training helps build you as a strong leader in your dog's eyes. If you find you are not securing success in training any of these items, please seek the help of a professional dog trainer who uses positive techniques.

The Drop-It Command

The drop-it command is taught by first giving the dog something the dog values, such as a chew bone. You then hold a treat right at the dog's nose and say "drop it." Ideally your treat is one the dog would rather have over that chew bone. As soon as the dog drops the chew bone, give the dog the treat. At the same time, pick up the chew bone. Once the dog finishes eating the treat, hold out the chew bone, say "take it," and hand back the chew bone.

Repeat this exercise. If the dog anticipates dropping the treat, hand back the bone and repeat the command without giving a treat. Once the dog drops it on command, you can award the treat. Only give a treat for compliance to your command, not when the dog takes action without a command.

Repeat the training a third time, then leave the dog with the chew bone. After practicing this for a few training sessions, if you notice the dog doesn't mind your taking that chew bone, don't give it back. Instead, set it on a counter. Then take out several treats and award the dog a jackpot of treats for letting you keep the chew bone.

Your dog will determine how much you need to practice this training. If the dog seems upset or resistant about your taking things away, you need to practice until the dog accepts your taking away the chew bone. If during any of this training the dog glances at you to give you eye contact, tell the dog "good" and reward the eye contact with an extra treat. Dogs giving you eye contact are looking to you as a leader, and this needs to be encouraged. However, if the dog glares at you and stiffens, the dog is defending the bone. If you experience this situation, consider getting professional help to train the dog to relinquish possessions.

The Leave-It Command

To teach the leave-it command, pick up two treats, one for each hand. Hold both hands out towards your dog, then open one hand exposing the treat. When the dog starts towards the treat, say "leave it" and quickly close the hand. Give the dog a moment to look at you. If the dog doesn't look at you after a few moments, encourage the dog by using the watch command. When the dog looks at you, say "good" and award the treat from the *other* hand—be sure not to give the treat from the hand you just told the dog to "leave."

Reload the hands and repeat this training. Practice the command with both hands so the dog learns that "leave it" means he can't have that treat when you say "leave it." When the dog better understands this command, he can learn to look at you right after you say "leave it," and you will not have to close your hand with the exposed treat. The first time the dog does this right, be sure to give a jackpot of treats as well as praise and end the session with that success.

Using a Release Word

A release word is used to let the dog know the task is ended. For example, when I tell the dog to wait, I expect the dog to do so until I give a release word. Some examples of release words are "okay" or "free." If I tell the dog "good," I am trying to communicate the dog is doing things correctly. The word "good" doesn't mean stop doing things, but for the dog to keep up the good work.

Real Life Adventures with Drop-It and Leave-It

Since my property is a few acres and we have horses, I am often using either drop-it or leave-it commands since dogs have a hard time resisting horse droppings, or what some people playfully call "road apples." If I see the dog go towards a road apple with his mouth opening, I tell the dog "leave it." If I discover the dog already partaking of an equine treat, I say "drop it."

Over the years, some dogs redefine their response to the drop-it command. When the dog hears "drop it," he seems to think if he eats faster and swallows quickly, it is okay. I know I can't allow that kind of insubordination, because if I do, the dog begins to think ignoring other commands is also okay. If you lose a round of drop-it or leave-it, you need to make sure the dog understands he must comply. To correct the dog, I go back to rehearsing the training for a few days in a row. This helps the dog choose to comply the next time. The sooner you begin this reversal after the dog blows you off, the better.

Impulse Control

A more impulsive dog can end up derailing your status as a leader. Those are the dogs who are more likely to decide to gobble down whatever you told them to drop. Often these dogs benefit from impulse control training more than other dogs, but there is a value to doing this training with all dogs. Dogs who learn impulse control can learn to stop an action they've already set their mind to doing.

To teach impulse control, first attach a long leash to the dog. Have the dog sit. Hold on to the leash, but don't try to restrain the dog. Toss a treat towards the floor near the dog and say "get it." Do this several times. After doing the get-it command five or six times, shorten your hold on the leash, then toss the treat and say "leave it." Use the leash to stop the dog, but don't jerk or reprimand in any way. The goal with this training is to teach the dog not to automatically decide what action he will take when you toss the treat. The dog needs to learn to listen to you, thus learning to follow your guidance even when the dog expects to act impulsively.

With the dog stopped short of getting the treat, have him come to you by reeling in the leash. Ask the dog to sit. Wait until the dog makes eye contact, then say "good" and award the treat. Don't let the dog get the treat you told him to leave; instead, pick it up. Practice the leave-it command a few more times, then give the dog a break. Do the get-it and leave-it command practices until the dog no longer needs the leash to stop, only your verbal command.

Possessive Dogs and Sneaky Dogs

Some dogs are more possessive than others. A dog being possessive over a bone will warn you off with a growl if you get too close. Some will snap at you. Dogs can be possessive about everything or selectively possessive. Common things dogs become possessive about are food, toys, sleeping areas, and even people.

Too often, people think possessiveness is a dominance issue. However, I've seen meek dogs act very aggressive over a possession. Possessiveness is an issue that can be seen in dogs at all levels of hierarchy. If you have a possessive dog, you will need to teach the dog that you own all of the resources. Training "leave it" and "drop it" is a good start. Don't hesitate to seek professional help if your dog becomes aggressive over possessions.

Like possessiveness, the tendency of a dog to be sneaky is also seen at all hierarchy levels. Sneaky dogs will walk away from trying to claim a possession if you or another dog is forceful about possessing that item. However, the dog will sneak back later and retrieve that very item. Although it is easy to envision a meeker dog adopting this habit, I've seen pushy and confident dogs be sneaky. For dogs, being sneaky is simply an act of employing a tool to get something they want. If a dog wants to eat but another dog threatens him, the hungry dog has two choices: fight or wait until the other dog isn't looking and sneak over to get what he wanted.

People who use harsher methods to discipline a dog rather than train for what they want can end up encouraging this kind of behavior in their dog. No one has to teach a dog to wait until you are not looking to do what the dog intended to do all along; it is part of the dog's instincts to do that. What this means is that punishing a dog to leave something alone has a high probability of failing. What works better is training a dog to leave it both when the dog knows you are looking and when the dog thinks you are not around.

If you have a sneaky dog, go into another room then peek around the corner. If the dog goes after something you told him to leave alone, repeat your command for the dog to "leave it." You may need to spy on your dog a few times and reinforce what you told the dog to break a sneaky habit.

Good Leaders Are Consistent

The suggestion to make sure a dog doesn't sneak behind your back and violate an order is merely practicing good leadership. A good leader makes sure the dog complies with the rules. Since punishment is often done after the fact, it isn't part of good leadership.

Moving a Dog from a Sleeping Area

Some people have issues with a dog deciding that he won't move from an area on the couch. The dog begins to protect that sleeping area or dog bed, and allowing this means you are not a very strong leader. If you have a dog who is reluctant to move from your couch or tries to protect a bed, you need to train the dog to move on command. One way to do this is to take a treat and ask the dog to jump onto the couch or lie on the bed. Reward the dog for doing what he was asked with a treat. Now, use a treat to get the dog to move off of the couch or bed. Do this on and off several times, then take a break and repeat the training an hour or two later. This kind of training creates a habit in the dog of moving off of a couch or bed on command.

If you have a dog who will not be lured from a place with a treat, attach a leash to the dog before asking him to move. Begin by asking the dog to move and hold out the treat. If the dog stays put, pick up the end of the leash and gently pull the dog away from that area. Give the dog a treat for moving, even if you had to assist. Now, ask the dog to go back up on the couch and reward that compliance. Once again, ask the dog to get "off" the couch. If you need to use the leash, do so. Repeat this several times, then leave the dog on the area at the end of the practice session as long as you asked the dog to lie there. That puts you in charge in the dog's mind. Repeat this training until the dog no longer needs the assistance of a leash to move. Don't fade the treat until the dog learns to readily respond to your command.

The Benefit of Your Dog Seeing You as a Strong Leader

I grew up watching reruns of the original *Superman* series that aired in the 1950s. When Lois Lane was in danger, she knew Clark Kent couldn't possibly help. He seemed whiny at times, not at all a strong and secure figure, and showed too much incompetence. Lois wanted Superman. Superman was a strong leader in her eyes, and with him, she felt safe. Those of you who are familiar with this story know that Clark Kent and Superman were the same person. Clark acted incompetent to hide his identity as Superman. Your dog needs to see your Superman persona, even if you don't always feel that way. A way to achieve this is by doing your leadership training and offering a secure tone of voice when the dog needs reassurance. Although some people wonder if dogs will love them when they ask for compliance, just as Lois came to love Superman, so will your dog come to love and adore you. By your becoming what the dog views as a strong leader, the dog believes you are a Superman and will feel more secure.

SABOTAGING SECURITY IN A FEARFUL DOG

Leadership, when done right, becomes a partnership where you both play a role. However, some people misunderstand their role as a leader when dealing with dogs who are feeling insecure. More timid and fearful dogs can often make us want to protect them. Although that is our job as their leaders, we need to offer the right kind of help when our dogs are afraid. The right kind of help brings security to the dog, whereas the wrong kind destroys it. When it comes to security in a dog, sometimes it is the people who need to be trained on the correct way to help out the dog.

Some people react the wrong way when a dog is injured. The wrong kind of fussing over a dog can create distress in the dog. Another area where people choose the wrong kind of response is when the dog is afraid. Actions such as scooping up the dog in a frantic manner, especially if the dog is not in actual danger, can create a highly fearful dog. Dog owners need to learn to allow their dog to deal with situations the dog is uncertain about, unless the dog's life is really in peril. Your dog needs to trust you to decide if something is a real threat, or if the dog can handle the situation with four feet on the ground. Once those feet are on the ground, you need to assist the dog in feeling secure.

Support for Insecurity

Jewel was a German shepherd mill dog rescue. At seven years of age, she was turned over to a rescue along with several other breeding shepherds. Jewel was deemed the most timid of the group, and although all of the dogs quickly found homes, Jewel ended up returned because she was too skittish.

I worked to help Jewel become more confident. One of the things I did was to do some basic training with the dog. Another thing I did was to take her for walks, which she absolutely loved. Doing things with a dog that the dog enjoys helps build a healthy relationship with the dog and can help to derail fearfulness. Although Jewel stayed by my side during the walk, she had a tendency to somewhat crowd me, reminding me of an insecure child holding on to a parent's leg. Unfortunately, I accidentally stepped on Jewel's foot one time. My first instinct was to rush to Jewel and wrap my arms comfortingly around her. That would have scared her all the more. My wrapping my arms around her would associate me with pain, not comfort.

I resisted the temptation to comfort her like a child and kept walking until she returned to a normal, stable gait. When she'd recovered from the unintended hurt I caused her, I got down to her level and rubbed her chest for reassurance. At this point in time, she was ready to be reassured. Before that she would have only associated me with the cause of the pain, and this already fearful dog would have become all the more timid.

As with most family pets, we tend to coddle dogs who become hurt. They learn through our attempts to comfort them that we are not part of what caused them pain. Still, this is not an ideal relationship. Mill dogs who don't have a good relationship with people won't understand our reaching out in an attempt to comfort them. Some more fearful and timid dogs, especially ones you've recently adopted, can have a similar experience. Although a dog can learn to accept comfort in a positive way when unintentionally hurt, it is far better to have an insecure dog learn to handle this issue by giving calm support like I did to Jewel. Instead of making a fuss over the incident, I gave Jewel the opportunity to build some self-confidence in being able to handle this kind of issue.

Keep in mind that the wrong kinds of interactions with a dog who is in an insecure state can unintentionally increase the fearfulness in the dog. Adding fuel to the fire is if you show excess concern while grabbing the dog, especially if your tone of voice counteracts security in the dog. Using a higher-pitched tone, especially while displaying angst at a time the dog is insecure, often causes the dog to feel tenser. You will have more success helping a dog feel secure by offering a calm reaction to issues and events when your dog has uncertainties.

Mistakenly Creating Fear

Let's work through a common hypothetical example of how people mistakenly create fear in a dog, which is the opposite of what a good leader needs to do. Let's say you have a small dog who is insecure. You are out on a walk, and you and your dog see a large dog approaching. You immediately snatch up your dog. Let's make this situation worse: Let's have you be apprehensive while you do this and talk to the dog with a touch of angst in your voice as you coddle the dog saying "It's okay." The next time a dog approaches, your dog will probably halt and may cower. This now triggers you to again quickly snatch up the dog and use what you feel is a soothing technique, but your tone is an octave too high to convey security in any dog. Soon your dog has learned to look to you with painfully fearful eyes every time the dog is uncertain, and you have learned to respond by picking up the dog, thus supporting a fear cycle in the dog. Dogs looking to you in this manner are not looking to you as a leader, they are looking for you to rescue them. The problem is that a lot of the time, the dog learns to do this when he is not in danger.

Now, let's look at the right way to do things. You see a dog approaching. You don't change your pace or react to the dog, because you are just watching to make sure that dog is going to be amiable. As the dog gets closer, you become a little less certain that this dog is as amiable as you'd like, because the dog is staring too intently at your dog. If you have time, step in between the approaching dog and your dog. In a calm voice tell your dog "up." Your dog is already trained that this means you are going to pick up and carry the dog. Since you did this training when there were no dogs around, your dog doesn't automatically think this is a fearful situation. Your calm tone of voice also conveys there is not necessarily a threat.

Teaching the Up Command

As good leaders, we sometimes need to protect the dog. Small dogs in particular can be vulnerable to injury from uncontrolled off-leash dogs. If you think your dog is in danger from another dog, by all means pick up your dog. But, there is a correct way to do this and an incorrect way. Snatching up a dog when you are feeling panicked can scare a dog all the more. Your anxious actions can generate more fearfulness in a dog. This can actually train a dog to become afraid of other dogs, even those that are not a threat. A better way to pick up the dog is to use a command such as "up" and then calmly pick up the dog. Since this is done in a calm fashion that doesn't upset the dog, there is no problem if you err on the side of caution.

When you first teach the up command, practice doing the command inside your house. Practice stepping and not stepping in front of the dog when doing the up command. State the command "up" and then calmly pick up the dog. Hold the dog until the dog becomes calm and secure. After the dog learns to associate the up command with being picked up and feeling secure, begin to pick up the dog more quickly, but make sure the dog completely settles down afterwards. Once that is accomplished, you can more quickly pick up the dog and carry him a short distance, just like you may have to do in a threatening situation. The key during these practices is to make sure that the dog settles down and relaxes after you pick him up.

Once you train the dog to feel secure inside your house, practice picking up the dog outside, when there is no threat. Part of the practice is for you as well as the dog. You need to learn how to pick up a dog in a secure manner as well as act calm when you use the up command. This way the two of you become a team about feeling secure. Don't forget to practice picking the dog up quickly, and to use the up command every time, as well as stepping in front and not stepping in front of the dog. The goal is to teach the dog that "up" means the dog will be picked up, sometimes quickly, but will calm down afterwards.

CHAPTER 10
Desensitizing Fears

Desensitization is a technique to deal with fear. There are specific steps to secure success, including rules for repetition and the role of counter-conditioning. Even when you understand the principles of desensitization, specific examples are always helpful, such as when you go to clip your dog's nails. Sometimes traditional desensitization just doesn't seem to help a dog. One reason is when the dog is responding to what can be called additive fear effects. Understanding what creates this issue and how to correctly deal with the situation can help dog owners learn to extinguish unwanted fear responses.

DEFINING TERMS
Several terms used in this chapter are defined below:

- **Conditioned response** is a learned response to the previously neutral stimulus.

- **Counter-conditioning** is a process in which you teach the dog a positive association towards something the dog has developed a negative association with.

- **Desensitizing** is a process in which you cause a dog to have less of a reaction towards something.

- **Stimulus** is something causing or regarded as causing a response.

161

- **Negative stimulus** is a stimulus with undesirable consequences.

- **Trigger** is an event that precipitates other events.

STEPS FOR DESENSITIZATION

There are three steps to desensitization. They include identifying the trigger, teaching a coping mechanism, and teaching the dog to learn to use the coping mechanism to get over being upset.

Step One: Identify What Is Upsetting the Dog

In this hypothetical example, we will look at desensitizing the sound of a doorbell. The doorbell sound has become a trigger for our sample dog. That means as soon as the sound is heard, the dog becomes very afraid. This probably came about because the dog was noise sensitive. Noise-sensitive dogs often become fearful about noises unless their owner helps them learn to cope. The more the dog hears the noise, the more the dog learns to associate that noise with fear. To change that pattern, the dog needs to be desensitized to the noise. The first step to doing this is identifying that the dog has an adverse reaction to the noise of the doorbell and that sound triggers the dog's fear.

Step Two: Teach a Coping Mechanism

In step two, you teach the dog how to relax on cue. One way to do that is to tell the dog to sit. Having the dog sit can later help focus the dog on you instead of the trigger, which helps in the desensitization process. Once the dog sits, speak a word or short phrase so the dog can learn to relax when he hears this word or phrase. An example may be the word "settle" or you may say "don't worry." Whatever word or words you choose, be consistent about using them. Also be consistent with your tone of voice. Use a calm tone when training and when using this tool in the next step. Be sure to practice your tone as you teach the dog.

To teach the dog a positive association with your choice words "don't worry," say those words and then give the dog the treat. Now, take a few steps back and again ask the dog to sit in front of you. Don't award a treat for the dog's sitting; instead, tell the dog "don't worry," then award the treat. Adding some additional training can help to secure the don't-worry command as a coping mechanism. That training is to teach the dog to look at you. So, after you practice the dog's sitting and learning that the don't-worry command is followed by a treat, add another step. Tell the dog "don't worry," but before you award the treat, ask the dog to "watch" or make eye contact. Practice this a few more times. Three times in the first practice is a good number.

Give the dog an hour or two break and practice this again. Only during the second practice, require the dog to look at you after you say "don't worry" the first time. Only award a treat when the dog makes eye contact. By the third practice session, the dog should look to you after you say "don't worry" without needing any cues from you. Don't hesitate to give the dog a moment or two to figure this out. Let the dog figure out that the reward comes only after he decides on his own to make eye contact.

You will want to practice the "don't worry" training often. When you practice, don't be too quick to award that treat. Have the dog practice waiting and watching you longer and longer each time. That extra time helps the dog learn to more completely focus on you and the task. The more you practice and the better the dog gets, the better the dog will be about coping with the fear trigger.

Using "Easy" as a Coping Mechanism

If your dog is good at relaxing with the word "easy" because you have trained that cue with the soothing touch, you can use that word in place of the words like "don't worry" or "settle." By following the training in chapter eight, you have already established a positive association with that word.

Step Three: Associate the Coping Technique

In step three, you use the coping technique with what is upsetting the dog. This is where you employ some counter-conditioning to the desensitization process. Since we are working to teach our dog not to get stressed out when the dog hears the doorbell, we will ring the doorbell, hold out a treat, ask the dog to sit to better focus on us, then tell the dog "don't worry." Once the dog settles down, you reward the treat. This begins creating a new habit in the dog. The dog can now learn that the sound of a doorbell is a signal to settle down. That is what counter-conditioning is all about, teaching the dog to associate a trigger with a positive response instead of a negative one such as fear.

Eventually you will be able to have the dog settle down without needing to focus the dog by asking the dog to sit. Often this begins with the dog looking at you when he hears the sound. Calmly tell the dog "good" and award the dog a treat. It is fine at this point to say "good settle down" and award an extra treat. However, even if you are very pleased at the dog's progress, don't use a motivational tone of voice. Keep your tone reassuring. Over time the dog will learn to settle down by himself and you can eliminate the treat. However, anytime the dog needs encouragement, feel free to offer your words "settle down."

Challenges Change Fear Issues

Dogs need to be challenged on their fear issues to help them conquer their fears and become more secure. You will find the most success when working to help your dog by learning how to challenge at a level where the dog can succeed. If the dog becomes too afraid of the challenge, the dog will regress. If the dog isn't challenged enough, the dog will not leave behind his fears.

RULES FOR REPETITION

Each dog has an ideal pattern for repetition of a training session. Over the years I've learned how to tune into what works for different dogs. The general guidelines are if the dog takes a long time to settle down after something upsets him, such as the sound of the doorbell, the dog needs more time before the lesson is repeated. For example, if the dog is having a hard time relaxing with the soothing touch, or getting a treat after the "settle down" command, don't try this again until the next day.

As the dog begins to learn to relax, start to do two practices a day, separated by at least five hours. Soon you can move to three practices a day separated by two or three hours. If the dog seems to settle down fairly quickly, repeat the lesson in an hour or two. If after repeating the training session the dog regresses, resulting in the dog taking more time to settle down, the dog needs more time between lessons. After this kind of occurrence, don't repeat the lesson that day. The dog is often helped after a regression by doing some routine training such as practicing the long down stay. This helps to return the dog to a more settled state of mind.

COUNTER-CONDITIONING

Some dogs can learn not to be afraid of a noise by using counter-conditioning alone. One way to do this is to record the noise, such as the sound of a vacuum, and in a controlled manner, introduce that noise while associating the sound with something positive such as a treat. When you play the recorded sound, you can adjust the noise to a level where the dog doesn't react. Play the noise and give a treat so the dog associates the noise with something positive. Provide the dog a few practices where the dog can associate this level of noise with a treat, then try raising the volume a little. Although the treat is a positive association, make sure the dog also relaxes. Some dogs will eat a treat, but do so somewhat nervously.

If the dog shows any kind of nervousness or seems hesitant about eating a treat, don't increase the level of the noise. Leave the level the same until the dog can relax. If the dog doesn't relax at that level, lower the level and see if the dog will relax. Once you achieve the dog relaxing at a lower level, stop the training for the day. You may want to lower the sound a little when you resume the training the next day. Only ask for the same level you had success with the previous day, then end the session. Stay at that level until the dog relaxes right away before trying to move up in intensity.

Once you resume your normal counter-conditioning, continue to raise the volume, giving occasional treats at each level. Allow the dog to completely relax at each volume level until you reach the noise's full volume. The key to success is to make sure at each level the dog has plenty of positive experience with the noise and learns to completely relax after hearing the noise.

Nervous Dogs Can Eat Treats

A dog eating a treat doesn't guarantee the dog is relaxed. Dogs who grab or quickly chomp a treat are still too nervous to go on to the next step. Make sure your dog is truly relaxed before considering your fear trigger diffused. Dogs who are relaxed will more calmly eat a treat. If the dog eats a treat and then goes back to fretting about or paying attention to the fear trigger, you need to do more work getting the dog to relax and may find using the soothing touch is part of your solution.

WHEN FEAR IS BEHIND CAR SICKNESS AND OTHER CAR ISSUES

There are a lot of reasons dogs get carsick. Some react to the motion of the car itself. However, if you feel your dog is getting sick because he is just too stressed about the car ride, there are several ways to try to help. My favorite is one that worked well for Shay. She was notorious for tossing her kibble when on a car ride. Shay typically got sick after a few miles of travel.

To get Shay over her car sickness attributed to being nervous, I found a way to give her a positive association with her car ride. Since this foster loved to go for walks and since she relaxed on those walks, I used that for her coping mechanism. I put Shay in the backseat for her car ride, but only drove a quarter of a mile. I stopped the car, attached a leash, and we went for a walk. Next day, we drove twice that distance before walking. Each day, I doubled the distance of the car ride before the walk. Within a week, she no longer got sick in the back of the car. Instead, she associated car rides with wonderful walks where she always enjoyed herself.

Albert got stressed when he had to go on a car ride, but he didn't throw up. Stress and fear can also cause a dog to need to answer the call unexpectedly. I was driving him to an adoption fair twenty miles away; however, in less than five miles the car smelled very bad. Fear had caused him to eliminate in his crate. I stopped and emptied the crate, rolled down the windows, and went on to the fair. The next time I was scheduled to take him to an adoption fair, I put him in the crate, drove a few miles, and we went for a walk. A short distance outside the car, I was grabbing a plastic bag to pick up his droppings. I continued the walk until he relaxed, then put him back in the car. Doing that a few times seemed to work for him, and he quit having accidents a few miles into a car ride. What may have also helped was at the adoption fair he got to hang out with some of his old mill dog rescue buddies.

During your training process, be sure to not associate the car with trips dogs may dread, such as trips to the veterinarian. Try to avoid this kind of situation until the dog has ample time to get over being fearful about car rides. If you can't avoid this, be sure to schedule several positive experiences in the days before and after this kind of event.

HELP, MY DOG HATES THE CRATE!

You may have noticed I often employ a crate as a training aid. Used correctly, this is a wonderful tool. However, sometimes people incorrectly use the crate for punishment or following a disciplinary action. When I picked up Shilo from the rescue, I was warned that she hated the crate. What they really meant was that for her, the crate was a place of fear, not security. Below are the techniques I employed to change Shilo's mind about the crate and get her to choose to lie inside even if I didn't put her there.

Use food to teach the dog to associate the crate with a positive experience. Begin by establishing the distance where the dog reacts adversely to the crate. To establish your dog's "reaction distance," select a special treat to use for training, something like a small piece of hot dog, which the dog shows more interest in than the average dog biscuit. Armed with your special treat, lure the dog towards the crate. When the dog realizes he is heading towards the dreaded crate, he may stop or turn away. Mark that turn-away area on the floor, either mentally or by setting down a thin entry mat.

Begin feeding the dog his meals just outside the area the dog showed a reaction towards the crate. The first time you feed the dog, lure the dog over to his food dish using that special treat, then toss the treat into the dog's dinner bowl. For the next feeding, encourage the dog to follow you to the mat when you carry his food dish. If the dog doesn't follow you to the mat, set down the dish and again use a treat to lure him to his meal.

Once the dog appears to have accepted his new feeding location by readily following you when you carry his dish, move the dish a little closer to the crate. To determine how much closer to move the dish, let your dog be the guide. If the dog took several days to follow you to his new feeding location, only move the dish a small amount. If the dog readily followed you the second day, try moving the dish a foot.

Once the dog learns to eat his meal right next to the crate without any angst, you are ready to move the dish into the crate. Place the dish just inside the crate, then put a special treat on the other side of the bowl so the dog needs to venture a little farther to get the treat. As the dog begins to show comfort eating from a food dish inside the crate, you can move the dish forward. It is a good idea to put a treat on the far side of the dish each feeding to encourage the dog to consider going a little farther each time he eats his meal. Any uneaten "special treats" tell you the dog needs to stay at his current level for a while. Any uneaten dinners tell you this dog needs to back up in his training to regain any confidence he's talked himself out of.

Once you reach the end of the crate with the food dish, you can go on to the next step. Grab that special treat and toss it into the crate. Tell the dog "crate." If the dog decides not to go after the treat, place a second treat at the mouth of the crate. Let the dog work into becoming comfortable with choosing to go inside the crate on command. Do not close the crate door yet. That part needs to happen after the dog decides he likes going into the crate.

When the dog is comfortable with going into the crate on command, change the treat you give him. Give the dog something that he needs some time to consume. I like to use a raw steak bone with scraps of meat still attached; however, a Kong with some peanut butter inside can also work. Tell the dog "crate," and when the dog goes inside, hand him this treat. Now, close the door. Stay next to the crate until the dog loses interest in the treat, then let the dog out. When letting the dog out, you need to prevent him from rushing out. This is very important because it isn't unusual for a dog who has a lot of anxiety about crating to want to run out as if there is a poltergeist inside. Be ready to grab that collar to make the dog exit at a calm pace. By preventing the dog from rushing out, you reassure the dog that he is not escaping a dangerous situation.

Some dogs will be so nervous from past bad crate experiences that the moment you close the door, they may show no interest in any treat. Talk calmly to the dog to reassure him, then continue your calm voice to tell the dog to "come along now" before you let him out. Be sure not to let the dog rush out. Make him exit at a controlled pace, even if the dog isn't very calm. If the dog reacted poorly when you closed the door, you need to back up in your training and work longer in the earlier stages until the dog becomes more confident.

Once the dog learns to calmly enjoy chewing away at a treat when confined in the crate, and to exit calmly when you open the door, begin leaving the dog for short periods of time after he has eaten. Be prepared to feed the dog his meals there for several months. Another way to get a dog used to staying longer and longer in a crate is to make the crate a place the dog prefers staying in. To do this, confine the dog to an area in the house with a hard surface, such as your kitchen. Take off the crate door so the dog can come and go freely. Put very comfortable bedding inside the crate. Some dogs get so used to staying in a comfortable crate, they will go inside their crate rather than lie on a rug.

The best way to have a dog learn to enjoy his crate is to give him reasons to want to stay there. Keep the crate experience positive for puppies by slowly introducing solitude. Make that crate comfortable and appealing for adult dogs. If you have a dog who already hates the crate, do your retraining slowly by working at your dog's pace. With the correct training you can make crating a pleasant experience that allows even a crate-hating dog to learn to like his crate.

USING CALMING AGENTS

A lot of people use calming collars (collars with calming agents infused) or calming sprays or liquid drops to help dogs who are stressed out when riding in a car or who may feel stressed when in a crate. This kind of aid can be very helpful; nevertheless, the calming agent needs to be introduced to the dog correctly to ensure success.

Frances Cleveland of FrogWorks produces the popular Merlin's Magic Calming Potion. She shares the correct technique to use these kinds of agents on a dog. Frances doesn't encourage people to spray Merlin's Magic or a similar calming agent directly into the crate, then shove the dog inside and hope for the best. She believes in introducing a calming agent to the dog first. To do that, you spray the scent onto your hand, then watch to see how the dog reacts to the smell. Signs of the dog liking the smell include the dog taking interest, moving forward, smelling more intensely, or licking your hand. With this kind of positive response, you can apply the calming agent to the dog as instructed. If the dog acts uncertain, spray the calming potion on a towel and place that towel in an area where your dog likes to hang out. This allows your dog to go to the towel containing the scent when he wants to. The dog can then self-medicate.

With dogs who learn a positive and calm reaction to calming agents, you can then use the scent in situations where the dog is known to become stressed. Keep in mind that with herbs or other calming agents, you don't want to force anything on the dog. You also don't want to apply any scents to the dog's nose.

FEAR OF CARS GOING BY

Some dogs will need training so they don't act fearfully when a car passes by. A good way to train the dog is to find a location where only a few cars go by, and where you can stand a distance away from those vehicles. When a vehicle comes towards you, turn the dog sideways to the approach. Some dogs will panic more if something unexpected and scary comes rushing up from behind or comes directly at them. Use the soothing touch to reassure the dog. Even if the dog gets a bit frantic, work afterwards to get him to settle down. Only do this training once a day until the dog learns to relax fairly quickly. However, try to do it every day to ensure progress.

Once the dog learns not to react to one vehicle a day, you can work to introduce two vehicles in a training session. Keep in mind that cars are often less intimidating than large or very noisy trucks, so pick your training area well. To do this training, you may need to go to a quiet parking lot after hours and have a friend driving a car help out.

Some dogs who are afraid of vehicles might respond to the redirect technique. When using the this technique, people typically ask the dog to sit, then ask the dog to redirect his attention to the handler. The "watch" command is often used to get the dog's attention on the handler. To ensure success, practice the technique before you need to redirect the dog so the dog learns the coping mechanism well. At home, ask the dog to sit, then use the "watch" command. When the dog does this, shove several treats, one right after another, into the dog's mouth. Some trainers refer to this as "machine-gunning treats."

172

Once your dog gets good at redirecting to you inside the house, go outside the house. Stay close to the house. Let the dog see a car moving on the street. Ask the dog to sit, and redirect his attention to you. Machine-gun treats and return to the house. After practicing this for a few days, you can begin to move closer to the traffic. Take your time moving towards the traffic. Make sure the dog learns to settle down at each level before moving closer.

Distance Matters

How far away a fear trigger is makes a difference. The closer the dog is to what scares him, the more afraid the dog will be. As you move farther away, you will often reach a point where the dog no longer considers that issue a threat. If you are having trouble getting your dog to relax about something that is scaring him, you may want to try more distance away from the trigger.

NAIL CLIPPING

For some dog owners, clipping their dog's nails seems an impossible task. Owners with this problem may ignore nails until they get dangerously long or may resort to taking the dog to a vet or groomer to have this done. Often, fear is why the dog resists this task. By learning how to correctly desensitize the dog to nail clipping, you can take the dread out of nail clipping. Unfortunately for some people, not only do their dogs hate this process, but the task has taken on a life of its own. The dog has learned to react to anything and everything associated with nail clipping. If this is your problem, you will need to first desensitize all the triggers the dog has about nail clipping before you can train the dog to amiably accept having his nails clipped.

Anticipating Triggers

When desensitizing a dog, the first step is to identify what is upsetting the dog. With nail clipping, there are some fear issues that you are better off anticipating before they happen rather than identifying after the dog becomes afraid. Dogs who are not used to your holding their feet and messing with their toes are more likely to become very afraid when you try to trim their nails. So instead of identifying the fear issue after it occurs, you are better off desensitizing the dog to things that commonly contribute to fear issues. Chapter eight talks about using the soothing touch to get a dog used to your handling his feet.

Desensitizing the Noise and Feel of the Nippers and Clipping the Dog's Nails

To begin desensitizing the dog to clipping nails, take the nippers (the same technique is used for a nail-grinding device) and hold it up to the dog's nail, but don't make any noise with the device. Instead do a little counter-conditioning by offering the dog a treat to get the dog to make a positive association with the clipping device. Repeat this action until the dog relaxes about the device touching his nail. Once the dog is amiable about this, rub the device on the dog's paw and then offer a treat. Once the dog relaxes about this step, move on to introducing the snipping noise.

To introduce the snipping noise, hold the device at arm's length from the dog. Now make one snipping noise, then offer the dog a treat. If you are using a nail grinder, turn it on, then turn it back off. As soon as the noise is gone, offer the dog a treat. Make sure the dog relaxes completely, then again make the noise. If the dog settles down quickly about the noise, you can begin to move the noise closer. Don't forget to treat each time. After the dog relaxes about the snipping noise close by, make the noise, then hold the device against the nail before you award the treat. Once the dog relaxes about hearing the noise, after which you place the nippers against a nail, you can make a snipping noise next to the dog's nail—just don't snip the nail quite yet. Give the dog several practices of getting used to the noise and the device next to the nail. Once the dog is relaxed about that, you can make the snipping noise, then flick the dog's nail. After the dog gets used to that, you can try snipping as described below.

My favorite way to clip nails is to use the same approach my seasoned dog-grooming friend has. First you secure the dog somewhere. Dog groomers often use a grooming table and tether the dog. With a smaller dog, you may place the dog on your lap or a small table. Use a tether so the dog can't jump off and get hurt. Begin with a back foot. Groomers have learned that most dogs are less resistant about their back feet. Securely hold the foot and snip the very end of the nail. Make sure you don't snip so much that you hit the quick. Groomers know that with very long nails, it takes a few days for the quick to recede so more nail can be trimmed. It is better to snip two or three times rather than quick the dog.

If the dog tries to pull back his foot, keep a secure hold on the foot and wait until the dog stops struggling. Then take one small snip. Be sure not to release the foot if the dog is trying to pull away. Instead, stop the trimming, just don't release the foot. Once the dog quits struggling, you can release the foot as a reward. If the dog is resistant at this step, find a successful place to end the session, then try again the next day. Be patient about conquering one toenail at first. Once the first one is successful, the work you do will bring further success. If you feel insecure about trimming nails, even after you desensitize the dog to the trimming device, ask an experienced groomer or vet tech for help.

Dogs Who Begin to Fret before You Try to Clip Their Nails

Once they become fearful of nail clipping, some dogs learn to fret in advance of the task. The dog cues off of the owner opening the drawer where the nail clippers are kept, leaving the dog's fear to grow wildly by the time the nipper touches the dog's nail. This often keeps the dog's nails from getting clipped. If you have a dog that begins to fret in advance of the clippers making contact with his nails, you will need to desensitize the dog to all those triggers that precede this task before you correctly acclimate the dog to nail clipping. If you are looking to clip a dog's nails for the first time, by correctly acclimating the dog, you will find that this is not a task for the two of you to dread.

Diffusing Established Nail-Clipping Triggers

Let's say the dog begins feeling stressed about nail clipping the moment you open the drawer to take out the nail clippers. You may note that the dog's anxiousness increases when you set the clippers on the table, and the dog tenses all the more when you put him on your lap. By the time you pick up those clippers from the table, the dog is ready for a full-blown panic attack.

To resolve this problem, you need to desensitize the first trigger the dog reacts to. In this example, the dog reacts when the owner opens the drawer to get the nippers. To desensitize this trigger, walk to the drawer and open it up, but instead of taking out the nippers, toss the dog a treat. Close the drawer and repeat. You may find it valuable to store treats in that drawer while training. After feeding the dog a treat a couple of times, take an hour break and repeat this lesson. Once the dog learns to think the drawer means treats, pick up the clippers, then toss the treat. Repeat for few times and take another break. Continue this session until the dog learns seeing the clippers means getting a treat.

You will use a similar process for carrying the clippers to the table. Once the dog is fine with that, you will put the dog on your lap and treat. Then you will pick up the clippers and treat until the dog no longer tenses about this action. With the nail-clipping process, the work up to this point is done to undo a negative association a dog may have already developed. Once that is accomplished, you can go on to desensitizing your dog to actually clipping the nails.

WHEN FEAR TRIGGERS OVERLAP—THE ADDITIVE FEAR EFFECT

Some dog owners who have dogs that get upset about the ringing of the doorbell may employ good desensitization techniques only to have them fail. In these situations, there may be more going on than a typical fear response. Dogs who experience an "additive fear effect" will often resist normal desensitization efforts. The additive fear effect occurs when a dog experiences two triggers that are close together. The net effect is that the dog's fear reaction becomes much higher than either fear reaction would be by itself. This kind of situation needs to be handled in a different way before the dog can learn to no longer be afraid of either trigger.

Understanding the Additive Effect

Almost everyone has experienced the additive effect of two fear triggers presented at an opportune time. Movies capitalize on this situation. In a scary movie, we are shown a situation that triggers a heightened fear level. Music is often used to build tension, and the camera keeps our focus as it moves down a hall in an apprehensive, searching mode. All the while, our mind tries to evaluate the danger. This first fear trigger sets us up. Then, bam! What just caused us to jump in our seats in the movie theater came from an unexpected source, not the issue we were focused on. Our heart jumps into action, our pulse races, and our breath catches. The net effect of us focusing on one situation we perceive as unnerving, then having a second fear trigger introduced, creates a stronger fear response than either would if introduced separately. Even when people go to the movies for fun, they can suffer a deeper fear from this kind of effect than they expected. Those people may have bad dreams afterwards. Others may be reluctant to return to other scary movies or places that remind them of the frightening experience.

Dogs can experience an additive effect from fear, which creates a much stronger effect than either fear stimulus does separately. Some dogs become unnerved by certain sounds. The sound of a doorbell can tense some dogs. If the dog is also afraid of people the dog doesn't know, you then have a situation that can create that additive effect of fear. The secondary trigger is a stranger the dog is afraid of who comes through the door while the dog is focused on the first trigger, that of the sound of the doorbell.

Here is how this may play out. The dog hears the doorbell and tenses due to the sound. While the dog is still feeling tense and apprehensive, the dog is often focused on evaluating the danger in that first trigger. Then, someone the dog doesn't know comes through the door, presenting a second fear trigger. Although either event in itself could scare the dog, the timing of the person coming inside the house while the dog is still working to evaluate the danger of the first trigger can have that additive effect. The result is that the dog experiences excessive fear, which often resists normal desensitization efforts.

What follows is that the next time the dog hears that doorbell, the dog's fear level quickly rises to a heightened level. That heightened level takes much longer for the dog to recover from than a normal fear trigger. Add to that the fact that the situation repeats itself when someone comes through the door after the doorbell rings. That second repeated fear trigger can reinforce the dog's fear. With each episode escalating the dog's fear, the dog may choose to begin to defend himself by biting the person coming inside the house. That became one of Kip's issues, a dog first mentioned in chapter one.

I've seen dogs become tenser when I ring a doorbell or knock on the door when I come to consult for a dog problem. For that reason, I often ask the owner to put the dog in a secluded area until I get inside the house and settled down. I did so with Kip, since he'd taken up the habit of biting people who came inside his house.

After three consultations Kip was showing good progress. He'd quit trying to bite me, and I was able to feed him treats and even scratch behind his ear. On that third visit, since I was only halfway through my time, I decided to begin desensitizing the dog to the doorbell noise and people coming over the house. I went outside, rang the doorbell, paused a moment or two, and came inside. Since Kip had recently eaten a treat out of my hand, the expected response was for him to settle down fairly quickly when I came through the door. I'd then feed him another treat or two so he could learn that the doorbell ringing and people coming inside was a good thing. This kind of counter-conditioning often works well.

That didn't happen at all. Instead, all the work I'd accomplished up to that point was gone. Kip was even more agitated than the first time I'd worked with him. It took me another hour of working with the dog before I felt I could leave on a more positive note. However, the situation was very far from where I wanted it to end. His excessive fear reaction, coupled with the large amount of time it took for him to begin to relax (he was still fairly tense after I left), tipped me off that I was dealing with an additive fear response.

Solving Additive Issues with the Doorbell

A telltale sign that you are dealing with an additive effect is that the dog is not desensitizing when you use normal techniques. In

179

Kip's situation, we should have been able to ring the doorbell, come inside, and offer him a treat. This kind of counter-conditioning typically gets the dog to associate the ringing of the doorbell and someone coming inside with a good experience, such as getting a treat. Kip's heightened state of fear didn't allow him to relax when he heard that doorbell. It took the dog hours to settle down enough to eat a treat. This makes offering a treat an action that comes too long after the trigger for the dog to make any kind of positive association.

If you feel your dog has an excessive fear reaction and is having a hard time settling down afterwards, you need to look for two triggers that initiated the fear response. Typically the first trigger tenses the animal, and the dog is focused on assessing the threat. The second trigger, when presented during that assessment time, creates the excessive fear response. The second trigger comes from an unexpected source, not from the same source that initially upset the dog. As mentioned, when you are dealing with the additive effect of fear, you will not have much success ringing a doorbell and then coming inside the house armed with a treat in hopes of getting the dog to see this as a positive event. Typically the dog's fear reaction is at too high of a level to eat even the tastiest of treats.

To resolve this kind of issue, you need to diffuse the triggers separately. Once the dog becomes desensitized to both triggers, you can then work to desensitize the combined triggers. However, when you attempt to reconnect the two triggers, you often need to separate them by enough time to ensure the dog begins to relax in between each stimulus. When working to diffuse these triggers, be sure to train one at a time, preferably every day. Don't work on the second trigger until the dog learns to settle down completely about the first trigger.

If your dog has an additive reaction to a doorbell like Kip did, the first step is to get the dog over reacting to the doorbell sound. A recording of that sound as described above is a good technique to use. Even if you can only make a little progress in one lesson each day, go at the dog's pace.

The second fear trigger for Kip was someone coming inside the house. Training this needed to be put off until Kip got over his noise fear issue. However, if you have a poorly socialized dog who is afraid of people, you can work on socialization of the dog in an area outside of the house. That will help you succeed when you go to work on people coming inside the house.

Kip's owner never came in the front door, but entered through a garage door. Kip had an established fear of someone coming in the front door. To change that perception, Kip's owners were instructed to use their child for practice. The mother was to send the kid out the back door and have the kid circle around to the front door. The child was to enter without ringing the doorbell or knocking. Once inside, the child was to offer Kip a treat, taking whatever time needed for the dog to settle down enough to eat the treat.

Once Kip learned to relax about the child coming through the front door, and after he got used to the sound of the doorbell meaning good things like treats, the two triggers could be put together. Kip already had experience settling down with a child coming into the house, so that was the best candidate for this step.

After the doorbell was rung, Kip needed time to settle down. Treats can be offered to the dog to help the dog settle down, and a cell phone can be used to signal when it is time to enter the house. Once the dog settled down about the sound of the doorbell enough to eat a treat, the child could then come through the front door and offer the dog a treat. If the dog didn't settle down right away, the child needed to be ready to sit calmly on the floor and wait for the dog to relax. People who have taught the soothing touch can use that technique to help.

What is key to success is to make sure the dog settles down in between each stimulus, such as the sound of the doorbell and someone entering the house. Practice is important. If the dog struggles to settle down, working on this issue once a day is fine. As the dog shows improvement, add more practices. Make sure the dog doesn't regress in training. If the dog does, go back to one practice a day. Don't try to bring strangers into the home until the dog is secure with family members. The best person to introduce when you are ready is someone the dog already knows outside of the family and feels comfortable with inside your home.

As mentioned, when doing this kind of retraining, the ideal situation is that no strangers come over to your house until the dog's issue is resolved. Unfortunately, real life doesn't always help out when working to reform fear issue like this. If someone comes over to your house before this problem is solved in your dog, call out to the person that you'll answer the door in a moment. Then, escort the dog to a crate waiting in a remote area of the house. It is fine to crate the dog the entire time the guest is over. You can occasionally excuse yourself, go to the dog's crate, and offer a treat and some calming attention so the dog learns that being put in the crate after the doorbell rings is a good thing.

DOGS WHO ARE AFRAID OF BEING ALONE
Fearful dogs who are very insecure are more prone to separation anxiety. With these dogs, the dog becomes so afraid of being alone that he panics. Dogs who panic will sometimes eliminate in the house when you are gone, even if you just put the dog outside. Some will tear holes in a couch or chew a favorite item such as a shoe. Some dogs are more silent sufferers and may pant and pace while the owner is gone. Punishing any unwanted behaviors can increase the anxiety the dog has, making a separation anxiety event all the more likely the next time.

Specialized training can help resolve this issue for many dogs. Often, the human needs to be trained to keep departures or arrivals low-key. If the dog has a habit of becoming distressed the moment he suspects the owner is going to depart, the dog can be desensitized to departure cues. Some of the confidence building discussed in this book helps a lot of dogs become more secure about staying home alone. For many dogs who have this issue, teaching the "I'll be Back" technique reforms the problem. That technique, as well as how to desensitize departure cues, can be found on the DVD *Separation Anxiety, a Weekend Technique* (available at www.peggyswager.com).

CHAPTER 11
Case Studies

Some of the work you do to help build a foundation in a dog that you will read about in this chapter may seem tedious. However, keep in mind that although a dog may occasionally need a lot of extra help, some dogs will make a breakthrough along the way. These examples are geared towards making sure owners who have dogs that need extra help have the information they need.

JEANNE AND WALLY

Jeanne rescued Wally, a four-year-old Cavalier King Charles spaniel, from a breeder. Wally was shown in conformation, but the breeder stated this stud dog didn't like the show ring. Once inside Jeanne's home, the dog seemed to settle in among four Burmese mountain dogs. However, problems arose when Jeanne tried to take Wally outside the home. She quickly discovered the dog was very reactive, then started to wonder if the issue was that the dog was extremely shy.

When dealing with shyness and fear in a dog, one of the first things I like to do is to assess exactly what I am dealing with. To do that, I first listen to the owner's story, then I see what the dog has to say. When Jeanne and Wally came to my home for our first consultation, I arranged to be the only other person in the room to minimize any distraction that might unnerve him. Wally escorted Jeanne inside the room in a quiet manner. This dog's calmness and willingness to walk alongside his owner made me suspect his issue was lack of confidence, perhaps from under-socialization, rather than something organic or due to soft dog issues. The dog had already drawn a sense of confidence from being with Jeanne and wasn't extremely watchful, reluctant to walk inside the house, or jittery.

I stood calmly in one place and asked Jeanne to sit in a chair. This tends to be a more relaxed position than standing, and some dogs are keen to pick up on how calm an owner feels; people sitting comes across to many dogs as a less worrisome position. Jeanne sat down and Wally sat beside her, then Wally glanced at Jeanne. Jeanne is no novice dog owner and knew to reward that eye contact with a treat. I recognized what was going on. Jeanne had taught the redirect technique to Wally. This is a good technique and can help some dogs, but Wally needed a lot more. He needed to learn how to feel confident from within.

I calmly stood about twelve feet away while Wally and Jeanne settled in. Then, I invited them to approach me. I didn't stare at Wally, but watched him indirectly. The pair stopped a few feet away. I talked to Jeanne, not wanting to interact with Wally until he decided it was time. He didn't take all that long to decide to step forward and sniff me, and then went back to Jeanne's side. This was my invitation to interact with the dog, so I lowered to his level and invited him to come forward. He came over expecting a treat. I had none, so he went back to Jeanne to get one, as well as to redirect his attention to her as he'd learned to do. I spoke to him, coaxing him back. He took a few steps in my direction, then went back to Jeanne. He didn't scurry back, but almost seemed confused. It appeared he was simply used to redirecting to Jeanne when uncertain, rather than exploring a person on his own.

I asked to take the leash. After a light pull on the leash, Wally came a few steps towards me, then stopped and wanted to go back to Jeanne. I didn't let him return to her. Additionally, I gave him a moment to realize what I was asking. He glanced at me, and I used the leash to coax him forward.

He stopped seeming comfortable at less than an arm's length. I lowered to his level, and since he didn't react adversely, I reached towards his chest, all the time watching his eyes and head. If his eyes had widened with panic or if he had turned his head sideways, I'd have stopped my reach. But neither happened so I rubbed his chest. An important thing to mention is that having him step towards me, rather than me just go to him, helps a dog feel more confident. A forward motion reduces fear; a retreat increases fear.

Wally was quite receptive to me rubbing his chest, so I continued until he relaxed a little more. Then, I went to his back right behind his shoulder blades. I began to work around his body using the soothing touch to get him to unwind. He did well on his forearm, and wasn't touchy about his back being worked. His tail was tucked, so after working along his back, I lifted his tail a few times.

As I worked on different areas on Wally, I calmly talked with Jeanne about some of this dog's issues. Since one specific issue Jeanne mentioned was that he didn't like his feet touched, I rubbed my way down the front of his leg, stopped at the knee, then returned to "home base," the place behind his shoulder. Since he did not react to the area above the knee, I rubbed my way back to the area below the knee. When my fingers contacted the area just above the paw, he lifted his foot. I didn't pull away from this but kept my fingers there, rubbing a time or two before going back to the area above his knee since he'd been relaxed about that. Had he not relaxed when I rubbed that area, I'd have gone to "home base" to reassure him.

Once he settled down, I returned to the area just above the paw. He didn't pull away this time, so I rubbed several times, then went back to above his knee. The next time I returned, I was able to work his foot. He only moved his foot a little. I lingered before returning to above his knee. I was pleased that he accepted my rub on his foot that second time. Since this was a noted problematic area (Jeanne stated she was shocked he let me do that), I decided this was a good place to end the lesson. One foot, one victory is a good way to secure more success in the future. It is best to end on a success, rather than push to a failure.

Considering how quickly Wally settled down during this first session, I was confident his issues came from a lack of adequate socialization when he was young. Jeanne supplied information indicating Wally may not have ventured out of the home where he'd grown up. When he did, it was to go to a dog show where the breeder placed him in a crate and pulled the wheeled crate around. The brief time Wally was out of the crate was in the conformation ring. There he didn't fare so well when shown in conformation because timid dogs are frowned upon. The breeder concluded Wally simply didn't like being shown in conformation. I suspect he was too under-socialized not to fret the entire time.

Jeanne and I talked over some of the things she was doing and some techniques to better socialize Wally. She'd been taking him to obedience class but just watching. This can be a good way to get a dog to settle down about a new place; however, the dog at some point needs to be nudged towards interactions at a level the dog can tolerate. If you only stay on the sidelines and don't challenge the dog (more guidelines in the sidebar in chapter ten), the dog may conclude that interactions are not safe. When looking to have a more timid dog interact, keep in mind that some interaction will not be safe. People wanting to work fearful dogs at a class need to make sure the human-to-dog and dog-to-dog interactions have a great chance of turning out positive. Otherwise the dog ends up more insecure than if you'd had no interactions at all.

Jeanne also took Wally to places like Lowe's to meet people. She noted Wally often wagged his tail when going into these places. She also noticed that when a forklift went by, Wally placed himself in front of her and watched from there. I told her that the tail wagging was from stress and not Wally being happy. The stepping in front of her was also something not to be allowed. I explained another way a dog can show stress about something is to step in front, walk ahead, or speed up when going towards something they are concerned about.

Stopping the dog from doing these actions can at times curb a dog from reacting fearfully aggressive. Not stopping the dog can lead to the dog becoming more and more reactive. If you halt the dog and get him to check in with you, the dog gets the cue that he needs to trust you that this is not a bad thing. The best place to halt the dog is next to you. You may also want to redirect the dog's attention towards you if possible.

Another problem Jeanne had with Wally happened at a bookstore. A man came up to meet the dog. However, when the man started to lean over Wally, the dog warned him off. Fortunately, the man picked up on the frozen-statue stance and didn't get bit.

My suggestion to Jeanne was to be very selective as to who meets the dog and how they meet the dog. If someone is approaching too quickly for Wally to tolerate, she needs to step in front of the dog. She may need to hold out a halting hand and tell the person this dog is shy. Ideally, the person Jeanne lets meet Wally is one willing to visit for a while, talking calmly so the dog has time to settle down about that person. Then the person needs to get down to Wally's level to make that first contact by touching the dog's chest. Wally would need to learn to become relaxed about strangers approaching before he could learn to let someone lean over him to pat his head.

We talked about watching for Wally's tail wagging. Wally did this before he went into places, which was a signal he was already feeling stressed. You don't want to introduce a dog to anyone the dog doesn't know when he is feeling stressed. Since Wally seemed stressed about every place he entered, the dog needed to first learn how to relax about going into places outside of his home before Jeanne tried any human or dog introductions.

Jeanne was in the habit of taking Wally to three or four different places to help socialize the dog. I suggested she choose one place at a time to build security. This process is begun by training the dog to feel safe in one place inside the store. That area becomes a safety "base." To do this, you locate a place, such as a quiet corner, where you are out of most of the traffic. A good place is where you have a wall to your back and where you can observe other areas without feeling cornered. Stay with the dog in that area and watch people walking by going about their business. Don't hesitate to use the soothing touch to get the dog to relax.

Once the dog relaxes about staying in his base, you can leave the store for the day. The next day you can return, go immediately to the base, and ask the dog to settle down and relax. If the dog settles down fairly easily, you may try a lap around the store. After that lap, return to the base, make sure the dog is relaxed, then leave. If he wags his tail nervously before entering the store, go to base, settle him down, and leave. Don't do any laps.

If your dog did well with the lap around the store, on the next outing, go into the store and walk around. If the dog is comfortable, go to the "base" corner and refresh the dog's concept that this is a calm and secure area. But don't leave. Venture into the store and meet someone. However, don't let people interact with the dog in the safe area. That area is not a place for challenges, but a place the dog learns to settle down when feeling stressed. Be choosy about who interacts with the dog and how. I prefer to have someone I know who is good with timid dogs do this first greeting in the store and sometimes invite a knowledgeable friend to help me out. Once you let the dog have a successful greeting, go to "base" to relax, then leave.

This may sound tedious, but what this exercise is doing is building a sense of security in the dog. To build a sense of security, you need to take little steps at first. That is why you start with getting the dog to first relax in one particular store, then getting the dog to relax about meeting one person. Soon you can begin to greet two people, then three. By doing things gradually, the dog has the opportunity to learn that if you are okay with the interaction, the dog doesn't need to be concerned. This builds a trusting relationship between you and the dog.

Once you get the dog comfortable meeting people in one place, move on to a new place. Do the same training in this new place until the dog relaxes there. Typically, you will find progress a lot quicker in the second place. Once the second place is secure, look for a third place. Along the way, a lot of dogs seem to find enough security that they no longer show tension when going into a new place, signaling that your training is concluded.

While this training involves people, you can do the same technique with dogs. I prefer to do people training first because I find it easier to control the actions of people. For that reason, you may want to begin this training in a dog-friendly lumber or horse feed store. After you get the dog comfortable with people, find a pet supply store and locate a "base." Once the dog feels secure, work on dog meetings. For the first meeting or two, you may want to find people you know who have social dogs. A lot of dog owners wandering pet supply stores are mistaken about their dog's amiability, and this can risk a setback with your socialization. Instead of leaving things to chance, consider arranging for a friend you know has a reliable dog to meet your dog. This way you can establish success right away, which allows you to build more success. Each success helps to build confidence in your dog. By doing this kind of a process, you have the opportunity to not only desensitize your dog, but build a relationship of trust between you and the dog.

What to Do If You Have a Setback

If you do have a bad meeting experience, be sure to not leave the store immediately. Instead, go to the "base" area and get the dog to settle down. If the dog settles down and relaxes fairly well, you may want to walk around the store at least once before leaving, but work not to greet dogs or people. Simply walk by them. Don't hesitate to step between your dog and an approaching dog to prevent the other dog from getting too close. When you step in between your dog and an approaching dog, do so as calmly as possible. The more matter-of-fact you are, the better. If the dog doesn't settle down at home base very well, work to get the dog to at least relax somewhat before you calmly leave the store.

The next time you return to the store after a setback, only ask the dog to walk through the store. Don't ask the dog to greet other dogs. Keep at this level until your dog walks around other dogs without showing concern. When your dog is able to go into the store without showing tension and pass by other dogs in a relaxed manner, again arrange for a "guaranteed" good meeting. It is fine if this meeting is with a dog your dog had a good meeting with before. For many dogs, repeating an earlier success is helpful. After the positive meeting, walk through the store. Before you leave, go to the home base and work to get the dog to relax. Once the dog is able to enter, move around the store, and meet one dog successfully, you can try working up in the number of dogs your dog gets to greet.

JEFF AND TATER

Jeff had dogs all his life. His mother also housed a variety of dogs as a foster. However, Tater was very different from other dogs Jeff had raised and trained to get along in his household. Tater was both very soft and very sensitive towards any kind of raised voice. As mentioned in chapter one, building confidence in soft dogs needs to be started when the dog is very young. Jeff didn't have that opportunity because he rescued the dog when Tater was around five months old. Since this dog came from a rescue, one might suspect Tater was already lacking in the correct training to help overcome the challenges of his personality. Fortunately Jeff's wife, Sheri, took Tater to a class to help teach him to comply with basic commands using positive techniques. This gave him a good start, but with Tater's more challenging disposition, he needed more specialized training to learn not to react adversely to the world.

Tater had recently turned a year old and was still struggling with self-confidence. Jeff wanted to take him to his mother's for the Easter gathering. Tater had been there once when he was young, but when dogs go through adolescence, they can change their perspective of the world. Tater was still dealing with artifacts from that transition. To help Tater have a positive experience at mom's house for Easter, Jeff was given some management techniques:

Jeff was to put Tater in a crate when the dog first arrived. The ideal place is somewhere that is somewhat secluded from the hustle and bustle, but not isolated. Allowing dogs to occasionally come and go as well as having strange people pass by while the dog is in the security of a crate can give the dog time to acclimate to the household. What you want to avoid is overwhelming the dog.

After half an hour, check to see if the dog has relaxed about this new place. A good way to check is to drop a treat the dog will likely eat inside the crate, such as a small piece of meat. If the dog doesn't eat the treat, the dog is probably feeling too stressed and will need more time. Don't remove the treat, but watch for the dog relaxing enough to eat the treat. Once that treat is gone, drop in another treat. If the dog doesn't eat the treat right way, the dog isn't ready to come out and meet the world. What you need to do is keep dropping treats until the dog becomes relaxed enough to eat those treats right away.

Once the dog is ready to come out, snap a leash on him. Lead the dog out of the crate and watch how he reacts. If the dog's tail is tucked or his body is hunched, take the dog to a quiet corner to sit next to you. You can use the soothing touch to help calm the dog. Be aware that the dog may require half an hour or so to settle down. Amiable conversation, watching television, or reading are fine activities to help pass the time.

You can venture out of your quiet corner after the dog begins to relax. Signs the dog is relaxed enough include the dog lying down, no longer yawning, and no longer looking around with anticipation or acting worried. Keep in mind that soft dogs often require training to feel secure with people and dogs they don't know. To allow the dog a positive experience, prevent people and dogs from walking up too directly, especially if those people make eye contact. If another dog is boldly coming towards your dog, step in between the two dogs in time to break off that direct approach. Dogs feeling too much pressure from a direct approach may try to flee or may strike out aggressively. Sometimes, if you turn your dog's body sideways to the approach, your dog will be more amiable.

Letting the dog become overwhelmed will work against the dog's feeling safe and secure. Activities that can also undermine the dog's sense of security include coddling the dog or snatching the dog away from a situation. Introductions where the dog learns to relax afterwards help build security.

Keep the dog on a leash while in the house until the dog feels relaxed. When you move around with the dog on the leash, keep him beside you. If the dog pulls forward, he may be feeling nervous. By insisting the dog stay by your side, that action can actually diffuse some of the dog's nervousness. If the dog is reluctant to keep up, work to encourage him to go forward. However, if the dog cowers, he maybe overwhelmed. If the dog won't walk alongside you because he is too afraid, return him to the crate. Give him some more time to acclimate before trying this again.

If you have several dogs trying to approach your dog at once, and this is part of what is creating stress in your dog, when you try the introduction again, only have one dog in the room. After your dog settles down about that first dog, add another. Let your dog settle down about each dog you add. After you have added five or six dogs successfully, you can begin to add two at a time. Although most people don't have access to this many dogs at one time, Jeff's mother is an exceptionally hardworking and dedicated foster. She typically houses more than twenty fosters. As for Jeff, I sent him with instructions to follow with this dog. Since he still struggles with the idea that his dog is very sensitive, he also struggles with taking extra effort with the dog, and like many dog owners, he didn't at first follow those instructions. Fortunately, having those instructions did allow him to create a system that did work for Tater.

The Adventure
When Jeff first settled inside his mom's kitchen, there were only a couple of small dogs there, so Jeff just let Tater loose. Jeff quickly noted Tater's back arched and his tail tucked. Jeff responded by putting Tater next to him until the dog felt more secure. Tater was beginning to feel a little less overwhelmed by the time Jeff's mom decided to teach Tater to use the doggy door going from the kitchen to the backyard. Working on training can sidetrack a dog from fear, and did so for Tater. Since the dog was beginning to feel a bit more secure, this was an okay time to try this.

In the backyard, a younger dog approached Tater and wanted to play. Tater hesitated at first, uncertain. Part of Tater's problem was he'd developed the habit of reacting adversely to dogs

195

rather than size up the situation to determine if there was an actual threat. With a little encouragement from Jeff, Tater finally understood the younger dog's intent, and the two dogs played until both were exhausted. That became the right experience for the rest of the visit, and Tater settled down, not worrying about the other foster dogs. Although Tater still needed work around other dogs, especially when on leash, this holiday visit helped to develop a good experience the dog could tap into in the future.

ZANE'S BOOT CAMP—BUILDING A MISSING FOUNDATION

Zane's mother was a mill dog rescue. The foster, Chris, whelped the litter of puppies, then decided to keep a little male she named Zane. When I met Zane, Chris had problems walking the dog along the street because the dog was afraid of vehicles passing by, along with other fear issues.

The first time I met Zane, Chris brought him over to my house. For a dog who'd been raised in a regular household, he was very fearful. Even after I worked almost an hour using the soothing touch, Zane showed little improvement. Part of what created excess fear in this little dog was Chris's attempt to help socialize the dog by taking him to a training class. The instructor really didn't know how to help dogs with fear issues and in her ignorance had made Zane's problems worse. Zane became so fearful that after a few classes Chris had to quit. I told Chris that she'd been very wise to withdraw the dog from the classes, but we both realized a lot of damage was done. This previously insecure dog had become highly fearful.

On the second visit to my house, after I worked with the soothing touch for half an hour, Zane settled down. I then took the dog for a short walk outside, going around my half-acre backyard. Zane was leash reactive to about everything, especially my dogs in their pen to the northeast of the backyard area.

I worked with him about seeing the other dogs, but only got him to settle down a little. I knew Zane had a lot of work ahead of him.

One of the goals with Zane was to get him better about walking on the streets near Chris's home. She wanted to work on that issue next, rather than keep coming to my residence for training. I met her on a street near her home where she typically walked Zane and worked with his reactivity towards cars by acting to calm him when the cars passed by. Although he reacted a lot when cars actually passed him, I showed Chris how to use the soothing touch to get Zane to settle down afterwards. Chris primarily worked with Zane at home base. Getting a dog to settle down and relax after something fearful happens can act to desensitize the dog to what is scaring him.

I'd gone to do a consultation to see how much Zane was improving and to critique Chris on using the technique. Although we typically met on the road where she commonly walked the dog, this time I had the opportunity to see how Zane reacted before he got to the road. I discovered this dog began to tense up the moment he stepped out of the house.

To help Zane become a more stable and less fearful dog, I offered to do a boot camp. A one-hour training session can quickly overwhelm a dog with all the changes you are asking the dog to do, even if those changes are good for the dog. A boot camp is done over three hours and allows the dog a lot of breaks in between smaller training sessions.

His first day at boot camp, since Zane reacted to almost everything outside my house, I planned on working to desensitize him a little at a time. Since he had reacted to the sight of my dogs when they were in a pen, I decided to begin there. I came out of a side door that was about seventy-five feet from their pen. Distance is a great tool when working with frightened dogs. The farther away a dog is from something that scares him, the easier it is to get the dog to settle down. Unfortunately seventy-five feet wasn't enough distance for Zane, and it took me far too long to get him to settle down after seeing my dogs in the pen.

Since the dog pen was northeast of my backyard, I decided to simply walk Zane around the yard for a while to help him relax. The walking area didn't pass by the dog pen. In general, I use walking a dog a lot to help with fearfulness. There are several ways a long walk can help a dog. Ideally during that walk, the dog is occasionally exposed to one or two fear challenges. The dog walker can help the dog learn how to respond to these fear challenges by keeping a steady pace and moving forward. The moving forward gets the dog not to dwell on whatever just frightened him, and the exercise more quickly dispels the fearfulness the dog feels.

Both Albert and Otis were taken on longer walks. Albert learned to settle down after a handful of one- to two-mile walks done over several weeks. Otis was highly fearful about everyone and everything, and he took a lot of miles. I logged some miles, my husband and son often took the dog for five-mile walks, and there were several seven-mile walks through a nearby canyon by my daughter. Fortunately, Otis never seemed that tired from the walks, and by the end of the summer, he had shown a lot of improvement.

I also understand that the average dog owner often doesn't have access to walking areas where a dog is less challenged, such as quieter trails. Many owners may not be able to log a lot of miles. Fortunately, Zane taught me a new way to help build a foundation of security in a dog without walking the dog about twenty miles a week for three months, as we averaged with Otis.

In my half-acre backyard, I began to walk Zane around and around. Unlike the trails where Otis traveled, this was the same old area and didn't have any challenges such as dogs, or bikes, or people passing by. There were also no vehicles nearby, which Zane still had some uncertainty about. My first thought was to

198

walk Zane for about twenty minutes, put him up for a break, and then do it again in the same area. Sometimes giving a dog a break lets him think things over, and doing the same thing again without challenging the dog can help him decide there is nothing to be afraid of, at least in that area. During my proposed twenty-minute walk, Zane made steady progress about relaxing. I decided to walk a little more, which led to more steady progress and more walking. Had his progress in relaxing plateaued, I'd have ended the session at that point.

After an hour and fifty minutes of walking, I needed a break and went inside to lie on the floor and rest my back. Zane lay right next to me. He panted at first (from his uncertainty, not from being hot), but over the half hour I lay on the floor, he finally quieted down. With only a half hour left of his boot camp, I took him outside for a potty run and lingered for about ten minutes. He then went inside and was placed in his crate until his owner came for him.

The next day (I like to do boot camps three days in a row) I decided to walk for at least the same amount of time in the same area, since Zane had settled down so well the day before. However, after about an hour of our milling around the backyard, my husband came driving by with a small tractor. I didn't mind because I figured Zane was ready for a challenge and knew without any challenges, he'd not improve. I fully expected Zane to react like he did with vehicles, and planned on using the soothing touch to get him to settle down afterwards. Then I figured I'd walk him until he completely relaxed, which would end the experience on a very positive note and help build his security.

None of my carefully thought-out desensitization to the tractor played out. Zane ignored the tractor. I was nothing less than shocked, though I didn't let Zane know. I acted like there was nothing to make a fuss over. However, this success gave me a new tool for my dog training. Typically, I use a lot of miles to help settle down a dog, like what was done for Otis. During those miles I introduce things that test the dog's security, then get the dog to settle down. This is a proven way to help reduce fear in an animal.

Zane taught me that if you have a dog who has never felt safe on a walk, you must first teach the dog to feel safe with you and with walking. A good way to do this is to walk in a selected area where there are no challenges to the dog. The repetition of walking the dog can help the dog learn to relax when walking with you. Once the dog begins to relax in one area, you can introduce one challenge at a time. As you conquer each challenge, the dog will become more confident in you. Then you can go outside of that selected area and work on learning to settle down while walking in a new area. Once the dog settles down, he can again take on challenges. Although this is tedious, it works for dogs who are very afraid and very reactive on walks.

The key to success is repetition and timing. Zane felt somewhat insecure in my backyard, but not overwhelmed. Together, we had trodden around my backyard for a long time, giving him time to feel relaxed when walking with me. By the time we had the unexpected "tractor challenge," he felt secure enough walking with me not to react. With the tractor success at hand, I decided to walk over to my two dogs in their pen. Zane, for once, didn't lunge at them when on the leash.

I instructed Chris to continue Zane's reform by finding a fairly quiet path instead of walking along the street. I also told her not to plan on walking for half an hour, then turn back to home. Instead, she was to go a short distance, perhaps an eighth of a mile, then come back the same way. I wanted her to repeat going back and forth on this path for her normal hour walk. I said after two or three passes, if Zane wasn't settling down, to reduce the distance by half. She was to do this for however many days it took for Zane to feel very relaxed about that part of the path.

I also coached Chris to try to do this walking at a time when she and Zane were less likely to encounter other people or dogs. Once the dog learned to relax about that first eighth of a mile, she could walk when they were more likely to encounter other people, dogs, and bikes. As soon as Zane relaxed about those challenges, Chris could begin to extend the distance a little at a time. This did the trick for Zane. He learned to become less fearful when on walks.

Zane taught me that with some highly fearful dogs, what is more important than miles is repetition. If you have a dog who can't seem to relax during a walk, especially if that walk is a longer walk, try going over a small area again and again. Even if all you do is go down your driveway to your street, then turn around and go back, this may be where you need to start. Be sure to choose a time when there is nothing coming down your street to scare the dog. You can keep a watch out for approaching vehicles, dogs, people, and bikes. When you see them coming, simply walk in small circles, five to ten feet in diameter, near the front of your house. Once this challenge has passed, resume your walk towards the street.

Do this as many days as it takes for the dog to learn to relax about that area. Then you can begin to expand the area where you walk, just doing so gradually. Keep in mind that if you encounter something that scares the dog, you will need to repeat walking that area until the dog again learns to relax. You also need to make sure you don't speed up when walking away from a challenge. As well, be sure to end the lesson at a point where the dog is relaxed rather than tense.

EPILOGUE

The other day I was rummaging around in some dog supplies when I heard a rattle. I reached down and found a small prescription container of "doggy downers." Otis and Albert had arrived at my house with those pills since they'd been on them at the kennel. I never gave either dog any of these medications. I found ways to solve these dogs' issues through training instead. Both dogs now happily live in their forever homes. So do Emma, Jewel, and Shay. It is my hope that their stories and journeys along with the information contained in this book help you free your dog from fears.

EXTRA INFORMATION

CALMING AGENTS

I am very much against grabbing pharmaceuticals as a first step when dealing with fear and stress in animals. My first approach is using training, and I've had a lot of success where drugs have failed. Some people may find calming agents can help. In chapter ten, I talk about Merlin's Magic, a product offered by Frog-Works, www.frogworks.us. Additional calming agents to investigate include Bach Flower Remedies. There are several books on this topic, including *The Bach Remedies Workbook: A Study Course in the Bach Flower Remedies* by Stefan Ball. You can search for some of these books to help tailor your calming agent to your dog's issues. I have seen calming agents at times aid in retraining dogs who have fear issues.

READING YOUR DOG

This book talks about understanding our dogs better by understanding their body language. If you want to learn more about this topic, you'll find several book available, including Brenda Aloff's *Canine Body Language: A Photographic Guide*. Another book I feel most dog owners can benefit from is *On Talking Terms with Dogs: Calming Signals* by Turid Rugaas.

SEPARATION ANXIETY

A lot of dogs who are fearful are very prone to developing separation anxiety. For people looking to solve this issue, many have found success using the techniques in my award-nominated

DVD, *Separation Anxiety, a Weekend Technique.* For dog trainers looking to expand their skills, I have an accredited course available through www.e-trainingfordogs.com.

PICTURES OF ALBERT AND OTIS

At my website, www.peggyswager.com, I have links to the photo journeys of both Albert and Otis. There are pictures and sometimes video clips showing when I first got them, their original doggy RV, and the mill dog prayer, as well as documentation of their progress. Other dogs I've worked with may be included.

INDEX

ABOUT THE AUTHOR

Peggy O. Swager has trained dogs since the 1990s. She has written articles for *Dog World*, *AKC Gazette*, *Off Lead & Animal Behavior*, and many other magazines. Four of her articles won Dog Writers Association of America awards. Her book *How to Start a Home-based Dog Training Business* also won an award. She has produced a DVD on separation anxiety for dog owners called *Separation Anxiety, a Weekend Technique*, which was nominated for an award. An experienced horse trainer, some years ago she applied this expertise to working with puppy mill dogs at a local shelter, to great results. She now has a dog consultation business in Monument, Colorado, and specializes in resolving fear issues and difficult behaviors. Visit her at peggyswager.com.